RICHMOND
VIRGINIA

LOST SOULS RESTORED

African-American Interments
as Listed in the
Mt. Olivet Cemetery Register

1875–1908

Nancy C. Frantel

HERITAGE BOOKS
2011

HERITAGE BOOKS
AN IMPRINT OF HERITAGE BOOKS, INC.

Books, CDs, and more—Worldwide

For our listing of thousands of titles see our website at
www.HeritageBooks.com

Published 2011 by
HERITAGE BOOKS, INC.
Publishing Division
100 Railroad Ave. #104
Westminster, Maryland 21157

Copyright © 2011 Nancy C. Frantel

Other books by the author:

Chesterfield County, Virginia Uncovered: The Records of Death and Slave Insurance Records for the Coal Mining Industry, 1810–1895

Richmond, Virginia Uncovered: The Records of Slave and Free Blacks Listed in the City Sergeant Jail Register, 1841–1846

All rights reserved. No part of this book may be reproduced or transmitted in any form or by any means, electronic or mechanical, including photocopying, recording or by any information storage and retrieval system without written permission from the author, except for the inclusion of brief quotations in a review.

International Standard Book Numbers
Paperbound: 978-0-7884-5330-4
Clothbound: 978-0-7884-8790-3

TO

MR. JESSIE KING

MR. JOE JONES

MR. STEVE MITCHELL

MR. CURTIS SUGGS

Thank you for taking care of those who time apparently had forgotten until now, even though God never stopped watching over them and kept His loving arms around them.

A special dedication is also offered to Lucy Graham, whose grave marker had been buried and was uncovered while studying the hillside where she lay quietly for so long waiting to be discovered.

Table of Contents

Preface	vii
Acknowledgements	ix
Introduction	xi
Editorial Apparatus	xxi
Notes	xxiii
Register Front Index	3
Interment Entries	25
Appendix–Speech of Manchester Mayor 1878	139
Bibliography	151
Index	153

Preface

Richmond, Virginia–Lost Souls Restored, Mt. Olivet Cemetery Records as listed in the African-American Interment Register 1875–1908 ends the trilogy which started with *Chesterfield County, Virginia Uncovered, the Records of Death and Slave Insurance Records for the Coal Mining Industry, 1810–1895.* The middle book of the series, *Richmond, Virginia Uncovered, the Records of Slaves and Free Blacks Listed in the City Sergeant Jail Register, 1841–1846* continued the trail of human passage through history.

Beginning with the history of the coal mining industry using slaves as young as twelve, moving to jailed free blacks who were hired out for as long as fifty-nine years, and ending with blacks being buried one on top of another in a city cemetery, made the series feel like investigating individual crime scenes. Although taking place in different settings, all three books are bound by a connection to the Richmond, Virginia area and provide snapshots of history for a cumulative span of almost one hundred years.

Psalm 140:12

"I know that the Lord secures justice for the poor and upholds the cause of the needy."

Scripture taken from the HOLY BIBLE, NEW INTERNATIONAL VERSION. Copyright 1973, 1978, 1984 by International Bible Society. Used by permission of Zondervan. All rights reserve

Acknowledgements

Appreciation is extended to Jessie King, Joe Jones, Steve Mitchell and Curtis Suggs (the management and staff at Maury and Mt. Olivet Cemeteries). You patiently answered my questions and shared your knowledge of the hallowed grounds. Gratitude is also extended to managers Wayne Edwards and Larry Miller. Thank you all for your guidance, insight, and support.

Numerous archivists at the Library of Virginia patiently answered my questions and guided me to relevant material. Although I am extremely grateful for everyone's assistance, Chris Kolbe and Minor Weisiger deserve special recognition. Mr. Weisiger was especially instrumental in providing insight on the history of Manchester.

Storie Taylor Quast and Cody Chastain of Taylor's Structural Imaging, LLC also played a significant role. Your skill, understanding, and compassion aided in the "below the surface" effort to determine where those who deserved a voice waited to be heard.

Isaiah 40:31

". . . but those who hope in the Lord will renew their strength. They will soar on wings like eagles, they will run and not grow weary, they will walk and not be faint."

Scripture taken from the HOLY BIBLE, NEW INTERNATIONAL VERSION. Copyright 1973, 1978, 1984 by International Bible Society. Used by permission of Zondervan. All rights reserved.

Introduction

Richmond is located in the heartland of Virginia and was incorporated in 1742. William Byrd II, a wealthy Virginia landowner, founded the city. His family was originally from England, and he named the city after Richmond, England. Similar to its English namesake, the Virginia city was located along a river, the James River. Like many cities by major waterways, the river played an important role in establishing the foundation and legacy of the city.

Due to Richmond's proximity to this natural resource, significant commerce and growth were not far behind. However, the historical connection to the waterway brought more than just a means of transport; it brought a mindset. The channeling of power and wealth from England brought a legacy of oppression to many.

This legacy of oppression filtered easily into other communities. One of those communities was a town called Manchester. It was established just south of the James River in Chesterfield County on land owned by William Byrd [III] in 1769.[1] In 1874, Manchester separated from Chesterfield County through the legislative process and became a separate city.

Prior to the legal separation from Chesterfield County, an ordinance was passed in Manchester in April 1872, "forbidding burial within the town limits."[2] This at least explained Manchester's disinterment practice. Later in the Introduction other localities' practices are mentioned, and although legal, raise questions, including, "Has humanity really changed?"

It wasn't until 1874, that a Manchester cemetery was established. As reported by the *Richmond Enquirer* in March of that year, "The committee on the town cemetery have purchased a portion of Buck Hill property [once owned by Cornelius Buck, a native of Great Britain] for a town cemetery, and a force of men were put to work yesterday cleaning it up."[3] The cemetery was subsequently named "Maury."[4]

According to the *Richmond Enquirer* by August 17, 1874, several interments had taken place. "INTERMENTS.–The superintendent of the new city cemetery reports since its opening eight interments of white and two of colored citizens, and the sale of a number of sections. Under direction of an able committee, various improvements are being made and the cemetery is well worth a visit."[5] It is hard to determine exactly where the colored individuals were buried in 1874. The first entry in the "Colored" interment register for Mt. Olivet Cemetery was not until July 1, 1875. It is unclear if individuals were buried in the Mt. Olivet section prior to this record.

The separation of black and white is further evidenced by the Manchester City Council meeting minutes from November 12, 1875. The minutes document the purchase of the two separate registers. "Mr. Morrisett chairman Cemetery . . . also reported that he had purchased one interment book for the whites and one interment book for the Colored and also a record of Sections for each."[6] *Richmond, Virginia Lost Souls Restored* is the transcription of the "Colored" register.

More proof regarding the treatment of "Colored persons" is shown several years later in the January 18, 1878, Manchester City Council meeting minutes. "The following resolution offered at the last meeting by Mr. Gary was taken up and adopted. Resolved that the superintendent of the Cemetery be required to remove the body of the Colored person now buried in the white persons Divisions of the Cemetery to the Colored Division."[7] This resolution needs no explanation. An effort was made to find the individual's name, yet unfortunately I was unsuccessful.

Also in 1878, concern regarding the cemetery's lack of securely marked grave locations was expressed by the Mayor of Manchester. The minutes from the Manchester City Council meeting on March 15, 1878, provide an unforgettable impression of Honorable Jas A. Clarke. He clearly understood the importance of treating people with respect.

An excerpt of his speech to the City Council is provided below. Mayor Clarke's insight is significant enough, in my opinion, to warrant further preservation of his entire speech. The Appendix provides the complete record of the kind of legacy he left behind.

". . . I have lately and purposely visited Maury Cemetery, and am pleased to say that considering the small force employed the grounds seem to be remarkably neat and well kept, but I was surprised to be told by the superintendant that there was no plat of the grounds showing clearly and distinctly the location of each seperate section, it seems to me that this omission might hereafter lead to great confusion, as it often happens in locating graves in parts of the Cemetery not theretofore used, the superintendant is guided only by familiar knowledge of the grounds, a knowledge which it would be difficult to impart or to be acquired by a new or other officer, I was informed that a Surveyor had been at one time employed to do this particular work, and progresed so far as to make all necessary field notes and other preliminary materials, and that it would only required him about one month more additional work to have completed the survey and plat this surveyor was however suddenly arrested [stopped] in his work, and dismissed by the Committee or other proper authority on the score of economy as a useles escpenditure; the sections are now only marked by wooden pins which are too easily removed, and if removed difficult or impossible to be restored to their true places, these should be removed and replaced by boundary stones sus as used to mark the lots and streets of the City. I recommend that this work be at once resumed, and I presume that it could be done with les cost by employing the same engineer who has so much of the necessary material already prepared, and whose services can no doubt be again had . . ."[8]

    Manchester and the cemeteries were annexed into the city of Richmond in 1910, and remain under the city's watch today. During the period covered by this register, 1875–1908, Manchester remained an independent city. The "Manchester Cemetery" as marked on several earlier maps is officially listed as Maury and Mt. Olivet cemeteries now.

The unsettling trail to Maury was first traveled while researching for *Chesterfield County, Virginia Uncovered*. Along the way it was revealed that 226 "unknowns" (individuals apparently from the 1800s and probably included both black and white) were legally disinterred from Chesterfield County and reinterred in Maury. The individuals were moved the week of September 22, 1986, after being combined into forty vaults.[9] No gravestones or markers document their small field of rest by the busy road and railroad tracks.

Also discovered during the same research period were additional unknown individuals located next to one of the rows for the forty vaults. The public record states they were "removed from Property of Phillip Morris in Richmond, Virginia." According to the interment card, eight "unknowns" were reinterred on November 18, 1981, several years prior to the 226 "souls" disinterred from Chesterfield County.[10] Like their counterparts, they also lie in unmarked graves.

It was not anticipated that the last book of the trilogy would lead to uncovering more disturbing information about the same city cemetery. Both Maury and Mt. Olivet include areas where unnamed individuals are buried or where others had remains combined. Many of those interred in Mt. Olivet have a unique pain associated with them.

The disrespectful treatment of African-Americans is the theme in this summary. In addition to the previously mentioned Manchester City Council minutes, several original survey maps and Manchester Cemetery Committee meeting minutes were reviewed. This was done in an effort to obtain a better understanding of the cemetery's history. It was also important to conduct this research to better discern why the Richmond area's race relation issues still exist as of this writing, the 100th anniversary of Manchester's annexation with Richmond.

The separation of black and white persons in the cemetery was documented earlier in the Introduction. Additional evidence of the isolation of the "colored" section is clearly visible from its physical location in the back part of Maury Cemetery. Mt. Olivet was also eventually fenced in. On December 13, 1901, the City Council of the City of Manchester approved an ordinance to build a fence separating the white and colored sections.

"Be it ordained by the City of Manchester that the Cemetery Committee shall as soon as may be practical at a cost not to exceed One hundred dollars cause to be erected a proper fence in Maury Cemetery dividing the portion of said Cemetery set apart for the burial of colored persons from the portion of said Cemetery set apart for the burial of white persons and also cause to be constructed a proper approach or road to such portion set apart for the burial of colored persons from such point on Perdue Avenue or Green Street as said Committee may deem most judicious and that proper gates be erected at and on said approach or road and that the City Cemetery water supply be extended to said colored portion when the committee shall deem the same proper." [11]

The individuals buried in Mt. Olivet have their own story to tell through the register. Basic interment information was evident at first glance. Then disturbing activities were noticed in the register. A pattern of reopening gravesites for another individual to be buried in the same location was revealed especially during the 1902–1907 period. In some cases the person appeared to be a family member. A significant number of other entries provided an unsettling account of using a gravesite more than once, regardless of how long ago the original burial took place.

Although it is not the purpose of this summary to delve into the details of the case, the actions that took place during the Manchester City Council meeting on May 28, 1907, warrant mentioning. The minutes state, "The resignation of Wm M. Allen Supt of Maury Cemetery was rcvd and accepted."[12] The superintendent was responsible for both Maury and Mt. Olivet cemeteries.

In addition, the Manchester Cemetery Committee minutes from May 29, 1907, state that an investigation was to be commenced regarding the "late" (previous, not deceased) cemetery superintendent. The investigation authorized summoning witnesses if necessary. "Resolved that it is the [illegible] of the Cemetery Committee that the books and accounts of the late Supt. of Maury Cemetery shall be investigated and that such investigation be commenced on Tuesday night June 4th 1907 and continued from time to time until completed, and that said committee may summon witnesses and take evidence bearing[?] upon said investigations the services of a competent clerk to be secured."[13]

The trail of the investigation was not followed, however the excessive number of "with another" burial remarks stopped after this action. The last "with another" interment took place on April 8, 1907. After the suspicions regarding the superintendent were discussed, the register was void of recorded interments from June 8 until October 12, 1907, and the register's last burial entry was November 2, 1908. It was written on page forty-one and the remaining 155 pages were blank.

The white interment register was briefly reviewed and the observation was made that the practice of burying several people in one grave, especially children, was noticeable even prior to the 1902 beginning of questionable activity. A trail of "with another" interments was also noticed.

While working on the transcription it became increasingly difficult to match the surface evidence at Mt. Olivet with the information provided in the register. The documentation in the record showed up in some of the cemetery divisions, while in other divisions there was minimal surface evidence. The sections with unmarked graves were very troubling.

One of the divisions, located on the west side of Mt. Olivet, was labeled "Colored Single Graves" on the cemetery map. Some of the gravesites were noticeable, however there were no markers. The record indicates the majority of the apparent non-family "with another" burials took place in the division.

The second division of interest was located on the south side of the hill. Approximately 120 interments were listed in the register. Only two ground markers for that time period were observed.

While studying this area, an exciting discovery was made. The marker for Lucy Graham, who passed away in January 1891, had been covered up by dirt and grass over the years. She was listed in the ledger as being in a certain division, which helped validate the present day location of the same division as marked on the cemetery map.

The third division was also located on the south side of the Mt. Olivet hill. It was listed as "Colored Paupers" on the map. The register indicated approximately 375 people were buried there, yet there is almost no surface evidence.

The areas where individual gravesite indicators were missing shared a common clue. With the apparent constant disturbance of the soil over the years from hundreds of burials, the rocks and stones had worked their way to the surface. As a result grass was virtually nonexistent. It was as if the rocks and stones were speaking out for those below ground.

After questioning the best way to determine who, if anyone, was buried in several of the unmarked sections, I hired a company to conduct ground penetrating radar (GPR) on part of the areas. (Approval was received by City of Richmond Cemetery Office upper management prior to contracting the service.) This technology allowed images to be relayed back to the computer on the surface. After the data was processed and analyzed, the areas of disturbance or the more frequently used term "areas of concern" were documented. Being sacred ground, no soil disturbance took place using this technology which was management's and my absolute requirement.

The company representatives for Taylor Structural Imaging, LLC, drove from their office in Franklin, KY to Richmond and brought the appropriate equipment to conduct the test. My extreme gratitude to Storie Taylor Quest and Cody Chastain is beyond words. Their unrelenting work in the extreme cold was able to solidify what I was afraid of the most. The evidence did not show neatly placed individual graves in some of the sections.

The GPR technology provided cross-sectional 2–D views of hyperbolas, showing apparent interments typically lying three to eight feet below. The information was further evaluated and 3–D images of several areas were created. The color red was used as the contrast on the final pictures to document the "areas of concern" which implied ground disturbance below. In one image the pattern looked like blood was flowing.

Only a few sections that showed minimal surface burial evidence on the south hillside were tested due to the intense amount of data required to create a single map. The testing revealed significant areas of disturbance, however it is imperative to convey that this test cannot be used as an absolute determination of specific burials. It can be stated that a strong possibility exists that in the areas of disturbed soil there is minimal evidence indicating that orderly, respectable burials took place on the hillside.

Finding as much as possible about those buried in Mt. Olivet was important for another reason. While working on the book, it was discovered that the Virginia General Assembly eliminated the legal requirement to record deaths for the period starting midway 1896, and continuing until the first half of 1912. Although individual cities and counties could keep documentation if desired, it was not required by state law. Several localities kept records, however it does not appear that complete death records exist for all individuals listed in this register during that timeframe.

Considering this is an interment register, not a death record, it could be challenging to locate where all or even a majority of the individuals passed away. Therefore, it appears that this record is more critical than first anticipated. For those who may be looking for loved ones, this register may make that effort easier.

Almost 270 years have passed since Richmond was incorporated in 1742. The city has been the home of the General Assembly since 1780. Many citizens question how much has actually changed.

Consider the budget decision made by the Virginia General Assembly in 2010. Legislators voted to cut the financial support of the Indigent Burial Fund as part of the General Fund budget reduction. Money had been previously provided to the localities to supplement their care of the poor.

As a current example of continuing the mindset of the past, the Virginia Commonwealth budget cut made the care of the poor and oppressed more challenging for some localities. The City of Richmond representatives fortunately continued to finance the program using internal funds as of this writing. Government representatives for Chesterfield County, just west of Richmond, did not.

Efforts are being made in the region to aid in the healing process, including the wounds of slavery. Although now part of Richmond, early Manchester played a significant role in transporting slaves in the 18th and early 19th centuries. The slave vessels arrived and departed from the Manchester docks on the James River.

The riverbed route is now called the "Richmond Slave Trail." If the location of the trail is correct, the name may be a misnomer for part of the path. Slaves were loaded and unloaded on both the north (Richmond) and south (Manchester) sides of the river. In the early years of the trade, when the slaves were unloaded on the south side of the river, they apparently first stepped foot onto Chesterfield County soil.

Recognizing this painful legacy, regardless of which government locality owned the land and the docks, is critical in understanding the history that belongs to all in the area. Yet, moving forward has been a challenge. Spirited discussions regarding how to best document the history of the region continue to this day.

For some, healing is sincerely desired so we can be the community of one. As part of the healing, my hope is that soon it will be time for those who have been disrespected as evidenced in this register to be acknowledged, recognized and remembered. Neither the individuals buried on the hillside at Mt. Olivet, the 226 "souls" removed from Chesterfield County, nor the Phillip Morris "unknowns" have a memorial. It is as though they have been denied their very existence.

I hope one day their time will come and they will receive the recognition they deserve. The interment entry for a child in the register who never uttered a single word may have provided the loudest voice. The child died for "want of attention." (May 27, 1901 entry.) Perhaps the quiet hillside and the field of rest together will create a gateway to increased compassion, and this sacred cemetery will become the cornerstone of a new foundation for the Richmond area and beyond.

Matthew 20:16:

"So the last will be first, and the first will be last."

Scripture taken from the HOLY BIBLE, NEW INTERNATIONAL VERSION. Copywrite 1973, 1978, 1984 by International Bible Society. Used by permission of Zondervan. Al l rights reserved.

Editorial Apparatus

The register pages were officially listed as "Interments (Colored) in Maury Cemetery, Manchester, Va." The entries on each page were fairly straightforward.

At the beginning of the register was an index. The index, not to be mistaken for the book index, was written alphabetically grouped by page number only. The index at the end of the book is alphabetical per standard practice. Apparently when the "front index" was compiled notations were made in the actual interment record. These notes were written typically next to a name that was difficult to discern. This earlier "translation" activity is marked by using "NBN" meaning "Note By Name." In many cases the names were apparently interpreted correctly; however there are instances where a person is entered twice in the front index due to lack of handwriting clarity which skews the interment count if not taken into consideration.

In the transcription, entries are listed in the appropriate order according to the register headings. The columns are titled: Names of Persons; Age, with subtitles Years, Mo'ths, Days; Sex, with subtitles Single, Married, Widow, or Widower; Disease; Occupation; Division; Circle; Section; Part of Section; Number of Grave; Remarks. Years, months and days of the individual's age have been listed as "y", "m", and "d." Division, circle, section, etc. descriptions are in abbreviated format. The grave number is simply listed as "number" with the appropriate grave site listed. Remarks are listed at the end of the official entry, as positioned in the register. Information includes when a grave was "reopened" for another person to be interred in the same location, and some entries included the cost of burial. Normally the fee was $2.00 for a child and $4.00 for an adult. Paupers were not charged. All data has been separated by semi-colons.

Many times limited information was provided for the individuals. In those cases, the information for a particular category was not listed as "unknown" unless the register specifically made a note of the missing information. Due to the type of information listed, the phrase "cause of death" was used in brackets instead of the register column heading "disease" when there was a questionable entry.

The cause of death entries were copied as originally written. In some cases the cause raised questions. For example, on May 2, 1887, a gentleman was "killed by carrs." While the register writer may have meant railroad cars, the exact meaning was not clear and the entry was left in its original form.

Other bracketed information has been added to assist with ledger interpretation. As discussed in the Introduction, many times graves were reopened for burial of family members who passed away at a later date. In an excessive number of cases, individuals who showed no obvious family connection were placed in a grave occupied by another. If the "with (individual's name)" notation was listed, the burial information of the first occupant of the gravesite was included in brackets where traceable.

It is important to stress that this record includes the interment date, not the date of death. There are no official death notations provided for any of the entries, even though the cause of death is typically listed in this register.

Considering a major part of the time the Virginia General Assembly did not require keeping death records, the information took on a new level of importance. It is understood that historic registers of this nature typically contain many errors. My goal was to limit additional errors. A sincere effort was made to transcribe as accurately as possible to convey systematic, organized data. However, the transcription was not intended to be an absolute copy and is not guaranteed.

NOTES

[1] Weisiger III, Benjamin B., *Old Manchester & its Environs, 1769–1910*, 1.
[2] Weisiger III, 45.
[3] *Richmond Enquirer*, 3-13-1874.
[4] Weisiger III, 45.
[5] *Richmond Enquirer*, 8-19-1874.
[6] Richmond (City), Manchester City Council Minute Book 2, 1875–1880, 48.
[7] Richmond (City), Manchester City Council Minute Book 2, 1875–1880, 238.
[8] Richmond (City), Manchester City Council Minute Book 2, 1875–1880, 266.
[9] Frantel, Nancy C. *Chesterfield County, Virginia Uncovered, the Records of Death and Slave Insurance Records for the Coal Mining Industry, 1810–1895*, 18–19.
[10] City of Richmond, Virginia. Department of Recreation & Parks. Bureau of Cemeteries. "Unknowns." Maury Cemetery, Richmond, Va., November 1981.
[11] Richmond (City) Manchester City Council Minute Book 5, 1897–1909, 388.
[12] Richmond (City) Manchester City Council Minute Book 5, 1897–1909, 488.
[13] Richmond (City) Clerk and Council Manchester, Maury Cemetery Minutes, 1907–1910, 3–4.

Richmond, Virginia, Mt. Olivet Cemetery Register

[Beginning of interment record transcription. To assist with the history surrounding this record and the format of the transcription, it is advisable to read the Preface, Introduction and the Editorial Apparatus first. The summary below was written at the beginning of register prior to the front index and interment information.]

1,833
Interments
plus approx.
1300 interments
of slaves & ~~soldiers~~
on hillside

There was no date listed for the information above, no signature indicating the author or approval by a committee, and no other source providing reliability or origin. The notation was written in red colored pencil, while the original interment entries were all written in black ink. This accounting summary appears to be contrary to the actual interment record. There are approximately 1415 interments in the register as transcribed. An exact number may be impossible to determine since several entries were incomplete. The "1300 interments of slaves on hillside" appears to be unfounded. About 800 individuals in the register were born after the Civil War, leaving only 615 even possible as slaves. This primary source record appears to speak for itself. It is not known if other sources were used to obtain the figures of 1,833 total and 1,300 slaves. However, considering it was written in the front of this register, the numbers do not match up.

INDEX IN FRONT OF REGISTER

Index format: Last name, first name and page number in original register. The register page numbers will not match the transcription page numbers. Some names were listed twice by the original indexer. This action changes the total interment count and the second name, if different, is noted in brackets after the entry.

Allen Wilson, 2
Anderson James, 2
Anderson Sarah, Jane, 2
Ackerman Celia, 2
Adkins Willie, 3
Armstead Sally, 5
Allen Rachel, 7
Ambler Lucy, 7
Allen Mary, Infant of, 9
Adkins Maria 9
Allen Eliza, I, 9
Armstead Nerah 10
Armstead Josephine, 11
Allen Mary, 11
Allen Samuel, 11
Allen Jno R, 11
Allen Lena E, 12
Armstead Samuel, 12
Archer Henretta, 12
Abram Nahr, 12
  [also listed as Nahr Abram]
Armstead Francis, 14
Andrews Sydney 15
Andrew Daivid, 15
Allen Alfred, 16
Anster Octavia, 16
Andrews Martin, 17
Allen Eugene, 18
Anderson Roberta, 19
Archer Rubin, 22
Allen Lottie Belle, 22

Allen Sadie C, 24
Andrews Melvina, E, 26
Allen Sydney, 26
Armstead Robert, 28
Allen Margaret, 28
Austin Willis, 28
Armstead Lotta May, 29
Allen Mathews, 29
Anderson A, J, 30
Allen Lotal, 38
Andrews Sarah, 40
Anderson Sarah, 40
  [Andrews and
  Anderson are same
  person – listed twice
  by indexer]
Allen Lizzie, 41

Baugh Elizabeth, 1
Bell Mary, 1
Burwel, Parthemia, 1
Burwell Anderson, 1
Baugh Elizabeth, 1
Brooks Patsey, 2
Burk Thomas, 2
Burfort Lizzie, 2
Burfort Florence C, 2
Banks John, 2
Bland Cornelia, 3
Baker Welthy, Jane, 3
Bolling Matilda, 3

Booker Joseph, 3
Baker Mary, E, 3
Baugh Julia, 4
Boyd Eliza, Infant of, 4
Brown, James, 4
Baugh Stephen, 4
Bland Henry, 4
Boyd, no Initials, 4
Banks Martha, 4
Baugh Douglass, 4
Burch Bettie, 5
Brooks Lucie, M, 5
Burfoot Mrs Mary, 5
Burford, Mary, 5
Baugh Elizabeth, 5
Baker Martha, 5
Barcroff L, W, 6
Briggs Alexandria, 6
Baugh Sarah, 6
Booker Manola, Infant of, 6
Baugh Mildred, 6
Burfoot Mat, 6
Blackwell James, W, 6
Burfurd Ella, W, 6
Booker Willie, 7
Bailey Mary, Ellen, 7
Burford Carrie, 7
Burke Maria, 7
Barbelt Stephen, 7
Brooks Hilton Jr, 8
Briggs London, 8
Booker Mary, 8
Briggs Amey, 8
Binga Rhoda, 8
Bailey Alice, 8
Booker Luther, 8
Branch Mandy, 9
Baugh Mollie, 9

Booker Easter, 9
Branch Blanche, 9
Branch Eddie, 9
Brooks John, 9
Baker Mary, M, 9
Banks Nancy, 9
Bush Rebeccah, 9
Brown Frances, 9
Branch Mary H, 10
Baker Robert, 10
Burton Paulina, 10
Branch Woodson, 10
Brooks W^m, D, 10
Brown Lou, B, 10
Baugh Albert, 10
Baugh Julia, 11
Bruce Fanny, 11
Burrell Henry, 11
Bailie Elishel, 11
Booker Mary, F, 12
Brown M & M, infant of, 12
Bird Richard, 12
Booker, Russell, 12
Ball Alice, 13
Bentley Doctor, 13
Botts James, 14
Bennett, Edna, 14
Berryman, W^m, 14
Baker James, 15
Brokis Sam & Wife, Infant of, 15
Baker Henry, 15
Booker Harriett, 15
Bromskill Wesley, 15
Burnett Dixin, 16
Burfoot Arthur, 16
Branch J, M, 16
Burke Volley, 17

Burford Marcus, 17
Branch Lena, 17
Bruce W^m, 18
Brown George, 18
Burton Bessie, 18
Bradshaw Kate, 18
Bradshaw Kate, Infant of, 18
Baker Nannie, Infant of, 20
Bunton Rebecca, 20
Brigge Adam, 20
Bright Squire, 20
Brice William, 21
Barksdale Robert, 21
Bowman Lewis, 21
Booker Mary, 21
Brooks Louisa, 22
Barkdale George, 22
Booker W^m, & Wife, Infant of, 22
Brooks Otis, 22
Brooks Ada, 22
Brooks Stepen, 23
Brown J, M, 23
Baker Mary, E, 24
Bushby Jas, 24
Brooks Joseph, 25
Binga Anthony, Sr, 25
Barnes Mike, 25
Brooks Sam'l, 25
Branch Richard, Infant of, 26
Bright Elizabeth, 26
Brooks Lucy, 26
Bailey Eliza, 26
Booker Sam & Laura, 26
Brown Elizabeth, 26
Bacon Conrad, 27
Baugh Julia, Ann, 27
Bock Fannie, 27

[also listed as Rock Fannie]
Brown Augustus, 27
Blackwell Elizabeth, 28
Boyd Sally, 28
Brown Alice, 28
Blakey Joe, 29
Bowen Bessee, 29
Bullock Mittie, 29
Booker Blanche, 29
Baugh Jas, A, 29
Bollings Maria, 29
Brooks Alm Lee, 30
Brown Henry, 30,
Bundy John, 30
Bradley Edward, 33
Bacon Margarette, 33
Baker Abner, 33
Briggs Peter M, 33
Brown John, 33
Britton Blanche, 34
Branch W^m, 34
Branch Fred, 34
Branch Robt, Infant of, 34
Burk's Wise, 34
Branch Roswell, 35
Broaddaus, no Initials, Infant of, 35
Bailey Persy, 35
Booker Lee, Roy, 36
Bailey Andrew, 36
Bailey Alvina, 36
Brown W^m, 36
Bailey Hazel, 36
Bartlett Etta, 36
Bacon Conrad, 36
Brooks Mariah, 36
Brooks Henry, Infant of, 37
Booker Sam'l, 37

Ballard A, S, 38
Brooks Henry, A, 38
Branch Geo, Infant of, 38
Byrd Jennie, 39
Bland Hellen, 39
Baugh Elizabeth, 41
Brooks William, 41
Binga Rebecca, L, 41
Blackwell, Henry, 41
Baugh Cashelt, 41
Baugh Mason, 41

Clarke Mary E, 1
Clarke, Nancy, 1
Carter Robert, 1
Clarke Nancy, 2
Cole Bettie, Infant of, 2
Cheatham, Anica, 2
Coleman, Ann, 2
Cunningham Florence, A, 3
Claiborne Jane, 3
Carter Jacob, 3
Christian Walter, 3
Cheatham Amy, 3
Cox Joe, 4
Coleman Susan, 4
Chandler Roderick, 5
Coleman Jas, 5
Cassell Lucy, 6
Carter Eliza, 7
Christian, no Initials, 7
Coy Viola, 7
Clay J, H, 9
Coy S, Arthur, 9
Clarke Lewis, H, 9
Clayborne Martha, Ann, 10
Claiborne, Welton, 10
Cabbell Matte, 10

Christian Anna, 10
Coles John, 11
Cook Earnest, 11
Crampton Rebecca, 11
Coseley Hattie, 12
Carrington Ed, Paul, 12
Chapman Patrick, 13
Carington, no Initials, 13
Chandler Georgie, A, 13
Carrington Millie, 14
Colima, no Initials, 13
Carter Laura, Infant of, 14
Carter Joseph, H, 14
Chapman Ananiss, 14
Carter Payton, Infant of, 14
Claiborne Augustus, 14
Chatham Mary, Infant of, 14
Carter Rachel, 15
Cabell Sarah, 15
Chatham Martha, Infant of, 15
Christian Mary, 16
Cunningham, Henry, 16
Coy J, H, 16
Cox Sally, 17
Cox Ellen, E, 17
Colman Rosa, 17
Curttney Henry, 18
[also listed as Lirthey Henry]
Coleman Davie, 18
Ceasar R, & Wife, Infant of, 18
Copeland John, H, 18
Cooper Jas, Washington, 19
Coleman Nelson, 19
Coles Allen, Infant of, 19
Coleman George, 21

Richmond, Virginia, Mt. Olivet Cemetery Register

Cook Mary J, Infant of, 22
Crump Amanda, 22
Coy David, I, & Wife, Infant of, 23
Christian Nathaniel, 23
Coy David & Wife, Infant of, 23
Coates Virginia, 24
Cunningham Parthenia, 25
Crear Mary, 25
Copeland Algie, 26
Coles Marian, 26
Christian Lucy, 26
Coleman Algie, Davis, 26
Carington Mary L, Infant of, 27
Carington W^m, 27
Cunningham Eliza & Wife, Infant of, 27
Cole Mary, Jane, 27
Christian W^m, 27
Coleman Annie, B, 28
Cunningham Elizabeth, 29
Crampton Sallie, 30
Coleman Mary, 30
Coleman J, & L, Infant of, 33
Christmas Effie, 33
Cheatham Rayoman, 35
Crump Wilson, Infant of, 35
Coleman Hilda, A, 35
Clarke, Bettie, 36
Coles Allen, 37
Coles Langston, 37
Coleman Jeff, Infant of, 37
Chanler, Ellenora, 38
Clarke Prescilla, 38
Crump Willson, Infant of, 38

Clarke Minnie, Lee, 38
Clarke Willie, 39
Capers Noma, 39

Dixon Susan, 1
Davis Emily, 1
Dean Abner, 1
Dennis Archer, 5
Dickerson Jos, 5
Dandridge Kate, 6
Davis Edward, 6
Dean Edward, 6
De' Justo Carter G, 7
Dickerson Milley, 7
Davis Malinda, 7
Dandridge Henry, 8
Davis Henry, 8
Davis Alexander, 11
Dennis Betsy, 12
Davis, no Initials, 13
Dennis W^m D, 13
Dabney Joseph, 16
Dennis John, 19
Deane Carrie, 22
Dozelle Mary, 24
Drake Jas, 24
Dodson Wyatt, 26
Dabney George, 26
Davis Rosa, 28
Dunn Jas, 30
Dancey Brnee, 30
Deane Maria, 30
Dance Clarence, 33
Davis Pearl, 35
Davis John, 35
Dickenson Thomas, 35
Dangerfield Mary, 36
Davis Mary, 36

Deen Annie, 37
Dun Annie, 37
  [Deen and Dun are same person – listed twice by indexer.]
Davis Sarah, A, 37
Deane Lavinia, B, 37
Diggs Joe, 38
Davis Henry, 39
Davis Mat, 39

Edwards Ballard, T, 4
Edwards Mary, 7
Edwards Ethel, T, 8
Epps Martha, 9
Epps Mary, 10
Edwards Lena, E, 10
Elleott Merchant, 10
Erwin Ida, C, 12
Edge George, 15
Easters Alice, 17
Edward Lena, Infant of, 20
Eaton John H, 22
Eggleston Jno, 24
Edmuns Ema, Infant of, 24
Eaton John, & Wife, Infant of, 25
Edmons Cora, 27
Edmons Mary, Infant of, 29
Edleo Henry, 33
Edmons Henrietta, 33
Edmonson Vernon, L, 33
Easeley Bennett, 37
Edmons Joe, 40
Edmons, no Initials, Infant of, 40
Edmonds Isabella, F, 41

Fleming Bessie, 1
Flemming, Willie, 2
Finey Mary, Jane, 3
Flemming Mary, 4
Fleming Lewis, 5
Finney Artelia, 7
Fitzgerald Margaret, 8
Fowlkes Norman, 8
Friend Georgie, 9
Fife J, H, 9
Fountain J, & M, Infant of, 9
Fife Florence, 9
Foster Anna, 10
Foster Benjimin, 11
Fitzgerald Ella, 12
Flemming Ella, 12
Finney Charlie, 12
Finney James, 13
Foster Mrs Fannie, 14
Flemming Fanny, 14
Fife Heeman, 15
Fields James A, 15
Fields Martha, J, 16
Fields Isham, 16
Fuinir Joseph, 16
Flournoy Bosher, 17
Fergerson John, Henry, 17
Ford N, L, Infant of, 18
Fields Florence, W, 18
Furgerson Fannie, 18
Fowler Harvey, 18
Freeman Mary, 19
Fortune George, 19
Foster Horace, 20
Finnel Annie, 21
Foster F, Lee, 22
Fountain Geo, W, 22
Finney Cornelius, 23

Foster Carey, 24
Furgerson E, Esira, 24
Furgerson Major, Infant of, 25
Freeman Mary, E, 26
Freeman W, H, Infant of, 26
Fitz Carrie, L, 27
Flemming Garnett, W^m, 27
Fergusson Curtis, 27
Fitzgerald Catherine, 28
Foster Jas, 28
Flemming Emmit, 28
Fowlkes, Richard, 30
Fitz Jas, T, 33
Fountain Susie B, 33
Finney Annie, 33
Faisson Florence, 35
Fife Susan, 38
Fields Mamie, 38
Flemming Robert, 39
Finney Sarah, 39
Finey Adeline, 39
Flan Walter, 40
Foster Mary, 40
Fowles Robert, 41
Finney Bernard, Lee, 41

Goode Jas, Infant of, 1
Guthrie Charlott, 3
Goode Julia, 3
Gaff Jordon, 3
Graves Czar, 4
Garrate Wesley, 4
Green Anne Bell, 4
Goode Eva, 4
Giles Paulina, 4
Giles Alex, 4
Graves Ceasar, 4
Gibson Thomas (Townsend), 5
Gains Mary E, 5
Goode Rhoda, 6
Green Effie, S, 8
Gregory Susan, 9
Goode Laura, 9
Gibson Hannah, 9
Gray William, 10
Goode Joseph, 10
Glenford Emanuel, 11
Gizzard Isacc, 11
Glasgow Mary, Infant of, 11
Glassgow, Mollie, 11
Graham Lucy, I, 13
Goode Elizabeth, 13
Gibson Alice, Infant of, 13
Gisoni W^m, 13
Gibson Thomas, 13
Goode Alice, Bell, 13
Gaines Patsy, 14
Giles W^m, 14
Goode Joseph, Infant of, 14
Gill Josephine, 16
Griffin Adelaide, 16
Grun Littie, 16
Gregory Annettia, 16
Green James, 17
Green Beverly, 17
Gibson Mary, 18
Green Wavery, 19
Gordon James, 19
Gibson Mary, Infant of, 19
Goode Joe, 19
Gibson James, 20
Garland, Edward, 22
Goode W^m, & Wife, Infant of, 22

Graham Aley, H, 22
Green Betsy, 23
Golden Kathleen, 23
Goonele Jas, 24
Garnett Robert, 24
Goode Bettie, Infant of, 24
Gray George, 25
Gary Johnson, 25
Giles W, H, 26
Gordon Lee, 26
Goode Bettie, Infant of, 27
Green Jas, & Wife, Infant of, 28
Green Alex, 29
Goode Nettie, Infant of, 29
Goode T, & A, Infant of, 29
Graham, Florence, 30
Green Herbert, 33
Goode Eliza, 33
Gordon Lelia Isabella, 33
Goode David, 33
Grimm John, 33
Gray, Henry, Winfree & Bettie, Infant of, 33
Gibson Immanuel, 34
Giles Sydney, E, 34
Gipson Cora, Lee, 34
Goode Inez, 38
Graham Benj, 38
Gordon Annie, 40
Goode Robt, 41

Holmes John, Henry, 2
Hix Thomas, Infant of, 2
Howlett Jennie, 2
Haxall Josephine, 2
Hughes Genevive, 2
Hicks Lizzie, 2
Harris Ella, Infant of, 3
Harris Jennie, 3
Hughes Ida, Jane, 3
Hendley C, M, Infant of, 3
Haxall Sarah, Infant of, 4
Hill Ellen, 4
Hays Mary, 5
Heath Hattie, Infant of, 5
Harriss Elizabeth, 6
Harris Adaline, 6
Hewlett Mary, 6
Hughes Bessie, 6
Hall Lucy, A, 6
Harris Coleman, 6
Holmes Jennie, 6
Henderson Eugine, 7
Hudlett Abbey, 7
Hewlett George, 7
Hall Era, B, 7
Hunt Bettie, 7
Henderson Loula, A, 8
Harris Florence, 8
Hilton Amie, R, 8
Howlett Sarah, R, 8
Harris Lucy, 8
Hunter Sallie, Infant of, 9
Hill Charley, 9
Harris George, 10
Hicks Burrell, 10
Howlett Florence, 10
Hall Isacc's, 10
Harris Ida, 11
Hill Rosalia, 11
Henderson H, S, 11
Hicks Thos, 11
Howward Annie May, 11
Holmes John, 12
Howell Charles, 12

Henley Eva, 13
Harris Martha, 13
Hobson Estelle, 13
Hews Arther, 13
Hudson Mary, Infant of, 13
Harris Susan, 13
Harris Mat, 14
Hilton Fred, 14
Hilton Martha, E, 14
Hix Dolley, 14
Howard W^m, H, 14
Harris Mary, 15
Hayes Harvey, 15
Hatcher Sarah Anne, 15
Henderson Louisa, 15
Hewlett Louisa, 15
Harvey Nellie, 15
Henley M Susan, Infant of, 15
Hocking Floyd, 15
Harris Alx, 16
Hankins Johnnie, 16
Hall Francis, 16
Hill Estell, 16
Hayes Hezikiah, 16
Hilton Clara, 16
Harris Nannie, 16
Henderson Haninobal, 16
Holconber Jno, 16
Haden Emily, 17
Hewlett Thursday, 17
Harris Edward, 17
Hankins A, J, 17
Horks Catherine, 17
Harris Henrietta, Infant of, 17
Harris Henrietta, 17
Hunter Charity, 18
Hicks Amie, B, 18
Hilton Almira, 18
House Judge, 18
Howard Catherine, 20
Henderson Hannibal, 20
Henley Lucius, 21
Harris Preston, 21
Hankins A, & Wife, Infant of, 21
Harris, Sally, 21
Harris C, W, 21
Hankins Matilda, 21
Howlett, T, & Wife, Infant of, 21
Harris Lizzie, 21
Hix Johnson, 21
[also listed as Johnson Hix]
Harris Henry, 22
Hurt Jennie, 22
Hickman Ida, 23
Howard Mary, 23
Howlct Richard, 23
Hall James, 23
Howel Rachael, 24
Hatcher Jas, 24
Harris Robt, & Wife, Infant of, 24
Holmes Alma, 25
Hill Blanche, 26
Hays Ellen, 26
Harris Robert & Wife, Infant of, 27
Hopes Alexandria Benji, 27
Hill Mary A, 27
Hargrove George, 27
Haden Jas, 28
Hatcher Gladys, 28
Harris Chas, 28

Harvey China, 28
Hastings Sam'l, 28
Hilton Herman, 29
Height Mrs Martha, 29
Height Jas, & M, Infant of, 29
Harris, Nellie, 29
Hence Mary, 29
Hill Jno, E, 29
Hall Spencer T, 29
Haxall Jas, 30
Hobson Oscar, 30
Hughes Earnest, 33
Howlett Maria, 33
Henderson Landrum, 33
Hamlin Police, 33
Hilton Florence, E, 33
Harris Adam, 33
Howlett Peter, 33
Hilliard Sarah, E, 34
Hilliard Amanda, 34
Harris Robt, W, 34
Hackney Mary, 34
Holmes Mary, J, 35
Hall Lewis, A, 35
Hickman Roland, 36
Harris Moses, 36
Harris Mary, 36
Henly Chas, M, 37
Harris Neal, 37
Heart George, 38
Hill Oscar, 38
Henderson Albert, 38
Hobson Estella, 39
Hughes Bettie, 39
Hobson Lillie, May, 39
Hobson Willie, 39
Howard Louisa, 40

Harris John P, 40
Hanes Chas, 40
Harris Chas, 40
[Hanes and Harris are same person – listed twice by indexer]
Howlett Sousina, 41
Hill Elizabeth, B, 41
Hill Alton, 41
Howlett, Wilson, 41

["I" listed in index after "J"]

Jones Jackson, 1
Jones Armstead, 1
Jeter Joshua, 1
Jackson Henry, 1
Johnathan John, 2
Johnson Mary, 2
Jackson Martha, 2
Jackson Rebecca, 3
Johnson John, 3
Johnson Julia, Ann, 3
Johnson Robert, 3
Jefferson Elln, Joseph, 3
Johnson Grant, 4
Johnson Richard, 4
Johnson Indianna, 5
Jones Judy, 5
Jones Eliza, 5
Jones Chas, 5
Jones Julia, 5
Johnson Pearl, A, 5
Jenkins Isham, 5
Johnson Margaret, E, 6
Johnston Nannie, 6
Johnson Ruth, 6

Johnson Julia, 6
Johnson Susan, E, 6
Jones Albert, 7
Johnson Nancy, 7
Jackson Mary, 8
Jackson Susan, A, 8
Jackson Charles, 9
Johnson Tom, H, 10
Johnson James, 11
Jackson Mary E, 12
Jackson Emma, 12
Jackson Ruth, 12
Johnson Anna, 13
Jones Perry, W, 13
Johnson Susan, 14
Jones Lucy, 14
Jasper Mary, Alia, 30 yrs 15,
Jasper Mary, Alia, 21 days 15
Johnson Amelia Ann, 15
Johnson John, 15
James Herbert, R, 16
Johnson Charles, H, 16
Jack, C, 17
Jackson Nelson, 17
Jackson Antony, 17
Johnson Jennie, 18
Jones Nancy, B, 19
Jackson Ola, 19
Johnson Ella, 19
Jones Mary, 19
Jones Mariah, 20
Johnson Laroly, 20
Jackson Thomas, 20
Jackson Louis, Infant of, 20
Johnson W^m, H, 21
Johnson Hix, 21
 [also listed as Hix Johnson]

Jackson Rufus, 22
Jones Richard I, 22
Johnson J, Sarah, 23
Jenkins Willie, L, 23
Jones Agnes B, or R, 23
Jackson Mary, 23
Jefferson Davis, 23
Johnson Josephine, 23
Johnson Lelia, 24
Johnson Fannie, 25
Jones Robert, 25
Johnson Alexandria, 26
Johnson Louisa, 26
Jones Jacob, 26
Johnson Edward, 27
Johnson Lillie, 27
Johnson Lucy Ann, 27
Jones Willie, Robert, 27
Jackson Crenshaw, 27
Jones Sarah, 27
Jones Cl, 27
Johnson Joseph, 28
Jackson Horace, 28
Johnson Rosa, Infant of, 28
Jackson W^m, 28
Jackson Francis, 28
Jeemes Louisa, 29
Johnson Jas, R, 29
Johnson Mary, Royall, 29
Jackson Eliza, Jane, 29
Jones Jennie, 29
Jackson Eliza, Infant of, 30
Jones Tomey, 30
Jefferson Mrs, Anna, 30
Johnson Lousa, 30
Johnson Lewis, 30
Jeeter Henry, 33
Jones Dorothea, 34

Johnson Walter, 34
Jackson Thelma, 35
Jasper Cuffy, Jr, 35
Jefferson Chas, 35
Johnson Henry, 36
Jones Ony, 37
Jeemes Robert, H, 37
Jane Pinkee, Infant of, 38
Jones Lousa, 39
Jackson Roy, De'Witt, 39
Jackson Fletcher, 39
Jones Benj, 39
Jones Nancy, 40
Johnson Alex, 40
Jones Jas, 40
James Annie, L, 41
Johnson Robt, 41

Irvine William, 14
Irvin Elvira, 25
Irvine Leslie, 29

King Caroline, 2
Keyley Benard, 3
King Taylor, 3
Keeling Mariah, Infant of, 4
Keys no Initials, Infant of, 5
Key's Stephen, 7
Kuk Mary, 19
Keyes Calvin, 19
King Luellie, 21
King Sydney, 22
Kelly Nora, Infant of, 22
Keys Stephen, 26
Kinder Lelia, 28
Keys Ruby, 36
King Hazel, 38

Lewis Sarah, 2
Lives Eliza, 3
Lovelace Chas, 5
Lawson Emma, 5
Love Andrew, 5
Lipscomb Eliza, 8
Logan Josephine, 9
Logan Sarah, Infant of, 10
Logan Chas, 11
Logan Mary, Infant of, 11
Logan Al——, 12
Louise Roubert, 13
 [also listed as Roubert Louise]
Lirthey Henry, 18
 [also listed as Curttney Henry]
Lee Josie, 19
Langston George, 23
Lewis W^m, A, 26
Lewis W^m, 26
Lipscomb Green, 27
Logan Nancy, 28
Logan J, Louise, 30
Logan Mary, Infant of, 33
Locket Iseah, 34
Lewis Eliza, 35
Logan Zelina, 36
Laws Julia, 37
Love John H, 37
Little Arthur, 38
Logan Madelene, 39
Lee Edward, 39
Logan Robie, 40
Logan John, H, Jr, 41
Miller Eliza, 1
Mingleton Ellen, 1
Morris Eddie Nelson, 1

Moore Lelia, 1
Morris Emma, 1
Mayo Annie, 2
Mayo William, 2
Mayo George E, 2
Mayo Arroments, 2
Mayo William R, 2
Mariah, 2
Morris Tandy, 2
Mathews Hannah, Infant of, 2
Moore Adam, 2
Mayo Mary Ellen, 3
Monroe James R, 3
Mayo Jane, 3
Mingleton Walter, 3
Miller Victoria, 3
Mosby Robert, 3
Mann Nancy, 4
Morton Rebecca, 4
Morris Archer, 5
Mayo William E, 5
Mann Charles, 6
Meeborn L, J, 7
Miller Giles, 7
Morrison Ella, 7
Meller Sam, 8
Morton Robert, 9
Meekans Fanny, 10
Moosby Alfred, 10
Morton Amy, 11
Munroe Jane, 11
Miller Fanny, 11
Miller Ocolia, 12
Mayo A, Willie, 12
Mayo Rosa, 13
Morton Mariha, 14
Mann Georgeaner, 14

Montague W^m, 14
Morton Catherine, 14
Muse Joseph, 15
Muse Loti, Infant of, 15
Mayo Aggie, 15
Montague Carrie, Infant of, 15
Miller Anni, 15
Masse, E, 15
Mosly Powhatan, 16
Mayo Nichols, 16
Mosly Lucy Jane, 16
Mickens A, & Judia, Infant of, 17
Miller Kate, 17
Mason Lee, 17
Mason Estelle, 17
Miller Nelson, 17
Mason Sarah E, 17
Marshall Rebecca, 17
Monger Peter, 18
Montague Bettie, Infant of, 18
Murphy Fred, 19
Miller Adelia, 19
Milheres Rebecca, 19
Mosely H, & Wife, Infant of, 19
Moss Charity Ann, 20
Moosby Jessee, 20
Murry Chas, 20
Murry Antony, 20
Morton Thomas, 21
Mathews William, 21
Morton Tom & Mary, Infant of, 21
Meade Bennie, 21
Morton Amanda, 22

16   Richmond, Virginia, Mt. Olivet Cemetery Register

Munford Annie, L, 22
Mann Robert I, 22
Murry Emma, 22
Mason Delphia, 22
Marshall Matilda, 23
Muse Elvina, 23
Mayo Jessie, 23
Moore John, 23
Mason Mary, 25
Moon Lucy, L, 25
Meyo Sarah, 25
Murry Marie, 25
Miller Monroe, 26
Murray Gracie, 26
Miller Percel, 26
Miles John, 27
Mire Mary E, 27
Miller Peter, 27
Mann Thos, H, 28
Monroe Thos, 29
Mosby Chas, 29
Moore Gertrude, 29
Miller Olivia, 30
Munford Biunthel, 34
Mosby Arthur H, 34
Moseley Eliza, 34
Mitchell America, 35
Meyo Martha, 36
Marshall Frances, 37
Munford Earnest C, 37
Milles Elsie, 38
Mickens Albert, 38
Montague Mary, 38
Mosby Page, 38
  [also listed as Page
   Mosby]
Minus G, R, 38
Meekins David, 39

Moseley Chas, 39
Moosely Robert, 39
Meyo Ellenova, 39
Martin Mary, 41
Montague Martha, 41
Mason Henry, 41
Morton Robert, 41
Mason Henry Spence, 41

McKenzie Kate, 28

Nelson Frank Sr, 10
Narh Abram, 12
Nelson Cyrus, 14
Nash Charles Duval, 17
Nelson Charles, 20
Nelson Harrat, 21
Nelson Sophy, 22

OBland Harvey, 6
Orange Tom, 20
Olphin Granville, 26

Poindexter Louisa, 1
Potts Thomas, 4
Powell Willis, 5
Paine Clarence, 6
Peterson Elvira, 8
Porter Willie, 8
Peuchaum Bell, 11
Price Isac, 11
Price James, 13
Pool Thomas, 14
Pryman Addie, Infant of, 15
Perry Montrose, 16
Price L, L, 17
Page Mary, Infant of, 18
Powell Jeff, 18

Powel Chas, 19
Page Mary, 21
Parson James, 22
Pope Jas, 23
Price Rosa Bell, 24
Powel Cora B, 24
Price Joseph, 25
Prosser Nellie, 25
Powel Sissie, 25
Powel Eugene, 27
Patterson Ruth, 28
Patterson Sam'l, 29
Pinchane Dan'l, 29
Pascall Robert, 33
Price Geo, Allen, 34
Pride Bessie, 34
Powel Arabella, 34
Pennock Jas, 34
Pugh Florence, 35
Pery Jas, 35
Pollard Lelia, 35
Powell Glaydas, 35
Polk Lawson, 36
Pugh Roach A, 36
Pollard Annie, 37
Powell Mary, 37
Paraham Mary, 37
Page Mosby, 38
 [also listed as Mosby
 Page]
Pride Hellen, 38
Peasants W^m, Infant of, 39
Pleasants Howard, 39
Pollard Willie, 39

Quawls Samuel, 11
Quarles Peyton, 35

Ridley Richard, 1
Robinson Beverley, 1
Robins Elizabeth, 2
Randolph Walter, 2
Randolph Henry, 2
Randolph Mary E, 2
Randolph Wilson, 3
Revely George, 3
Randolph Lewis, 4
Ross Edie, 4
Reade Lewis, 4
Rollins John, Infant of, 4
Rawlings John, Infant of, 5
Robinson Emily, 5
Randolph Rachael, 5
Robinson Clara, 6
Randolph W, R, 6
Robertson Elizabeth, 6
Robinson James, 7
Robertson Priscilla, 7
Robinson Henry, 7
Ruffin Lidia, Infant of, 7
Robinson Pashal, 8
Reed Isaccs, 8
Randolph James, 8
Roane Daniel, 8
Robinson Coleman, 8
Robinson Sarah, 8
Ross James E, 10
Rudolph Martha, 10
Ross Chas, A, 11
Rudolph W^m, Henry, 12
Randolph Mary E, 12
Rollins Ella, 12
Robinson Emma, 12
Robinson Coleman, 12
Roberson Jula, 12
Roubert Louise, 13

[also listed as Louise Roubert]
Roane Kizziah, 13
Robertson Pittman, 13
Randolph Robert P, R, 13
Robinson M, & S, Infant of, 13
Randolph Lizzie, 13
Rieves Madaline, 14
Robinson Era, 14
Robertson Jas, 14
Ross Ruth E, 15
Robinson Delia, 16
Randolph Beng, 17
Randall Georgeanna, 17
Ross Mary B, 17
Ruffin Lilly, 19
Richardson Mary, Infant of, 19
Randolph Emily, Infant of, 19
Riley Adelaide, Infant of, 20
Robinson Floyd, 21
Richardson W^m, 21
Reed W^m, 21
Robinson Lelia, Infant of, 23
Robinson Granville, 23
Ross Jane, 25
Randolph Georgeanna, 25
Robinson Granville, 26
Ross Rosa, 26
Rhone M, Eva, 26
Roberson Rosabella, 27
Rock Fannie, 27
   [also listed as Bock Fannie]
Richmond Smith, 28
   [also listed a Smith Richmond]

Royall Jennie, 29
Rollings Maria, 29
Roane John, 30
Robinson Elizabeth, 30
Robinson Lelia, 30
Ross Virginia, 30
Randolph Ruth, 33
Richardson W^m, 33
Randolph Howard L, 34
Roberts Cyphus, 34
Robinson Charles, 34
Richardson Norvelle, 34
Roane Ora Roane, 35
Robinson Dora, 36
Robinson Laura, 36
Robinson Jas, 36
Robinson Joseph Henry, 37
Royster Jas, 37
Robinson Floyd, 37
Robertson Dilsey, 37
Reid Henry, 38
Richardson Grove, 38
Rock Fred, 39
Robinson John, 39
Russele Robert, 39
Robinson Fred, 41
Robinson David, 41
Robinson Marqurette M, 41
Robinson Ivly, 41
Robinson Linwood, 41

Smith Robert, 1
Stronn Julia, 2
Swoon Aaron, 2
Smith Delia, Infant of, 2
Stewart Willie, 2
Smith W^m, Infant of, 3
Smith Mary, 3

Richmond, Virginia, Mt. Olivet Cemetery Register

Smith Bertha, Infant of, 3
Smith W^m, 4
Smith Leray, 4
Smith James, 4
Saunders Mary, 4
Sydnor Frank, 4
Smith W^m, 5
Smith Alberta, 5
Smith Andrew, 6
Smith Robt, 6
Saunders Mary, 6
Smith Mary, 6
Stowe Cora, 25 yrs, 8
Stowe Cora, 4 months, 8
Scott Elvira, 8
Streets Harry, 9
Southall Maria, 9
Saunders James H, 10
Sutherland Miles, 10
Stepheny Matilda, 10
Simmons Richard, 11
Smith Peter, 11
Smith Hellen L, 12
Saunders Charles, 13
Simmon Mad, 13
Smith Joseph, 13
Stokes Mary S, 14
Schouren Aaron, 14
Smith W^m, H, 15
Sally Henry & Nancy, Infant of, 15
Smith Mary E, 15
Smith Annie, 15
Southall Oti, 16
Simmons Mary, 16
Saunders Lee, 17
Scott Mary Jane, 17
Stuart Emma, Infant of, 18
Smith Lizzie, Infant of, 18
Staples J, 19
Saunders Emma, 19
Staples Carrie, 19
Seigle, Mary, Page, Infant of, 19 [appears to be "single," not an actual surname in register]
Sharp Anthoney, 20
Stringfellow Peter, 20
Smith Linwood, 20
Smith Charles, 21
Scott Katie, 21
Starke Berta, 21
Slaughter T, B, 21
Strayghter T, B, 21
    [Slaughter and Stayghter are same person – listed twice by indexer]
Smith Lizzie, 21
Shelton Georgeanna, 22
Street A, 23
Statten Alexander, 24
Smith Amanda, 24
Scott Julia B, 24
Smith Lewis, 24
Smith Eddie, 26
Staples Estelle, 27
Smith Richmond, 28
    [also listed as Richmond Smith]
Sully Henry, 29
Smith W, & L, Infant of, 30
Smith Florence G, 30
Sneed Lizzie, 34
Stultz Norman, 34
Shaw Ophelia, 34

Street George, 35
Sterling Elizabeth, 35
Smith Mary L, 35
Semeoil Lelia G, 35
Sherron Thomas, 35
Simmons Louisea, 36
Smith Synthy, 37
Smith Pelio, 39
Smith Maria, 39
Stokes Berta, 40
Savage Lucy, 40
Smith Royal, 40
Scott Bessie, 40
Skipwith Ora B, 41

Turner Annie, 1
Taylor Mary, Infant of, 3
Trent James, 3
Taylor Jas, 3
Turpin Edmond, 4
Taylor Alice, Infant of, 4
Taylor Lucy, 5
Thompson Francis, 5
Tatum Ama, 6
Taylor Alice, 6
Thompson Blanche, 6
Taylor Geo, 6
Thompson Charles, 7
Thomas Rebecca, Infant of, 7
Thomson Ruth, 7
Twine Charlie, 8
Tompkins Maggie, 9
Thompson Laura A, 9
Turner Magr, Infants of, 9
Turner Granville, 9
Thomas Chas & Eliza, 12
Thomas Alice P, 12
Thomson Chas, W, 13
Thomalson Garland, 14
Tyler Osca, 16
Turner Eugene, 16
Thompson Ernest, 16
Thomas W^m, 18
Thomas Armstead, 20
Turner W^m, 20
Taylor Jno, 21
Turpin Armetia, 21
Taylor Robert, 22
Twine Elsey, 22
Timberlake L, J, 22
Trent Annie B, Infant of, 22
Taylor Archer & Wife, Infant of, 23
Turner Charlotte, 24
Turner Mary D, 25
Thomas Jessee, 25
Tubbs John H, 25
Threet H, & M, Infant of, 26
Thompson Eddie, 27
Turpin Edmond, 28
Tiniley Geo, & Wife, Infant of, 28
Taylor Paulene, 29
Threat Henry & Mary, Infant of, 30
Taylor Arthur, 30
Taylor Walter, 34
Terry Eliza, 34
Taylor Geo, Henry, 34
Taylor Catherine, 35
Thompson W, Y, 36
Tilery Robt, P, 36
Tinsley Leroy, 38
Trent Matilda, 38
Talleferro Custis, 39

Richmond, Virginia, Mt. Olivet Cemetery Register

Taylor Edna, 39
Taylor Archer, 39

Unknown Infant, no Age, 1
Unknown Infant, no Age, 2
Unknown Child, 12 yrs, 2
Unknown Infant, no Age, 3
Unknown Infant, no Age, 4
Unknown Infant, no Age, 6
Unknown Infant, as 21 days, 6
Unknown Infant, no Age, 6
Unknown Infant, no Age, 7
Unknown Infant, no Age, 7
Unknown Infant, no Age, 7
Unknown Infant, no Age, 8
[Page 9 in register lists unnamed person – not in index]
Unknown Infant, 1 month 4 days, 12
Unknown Female, 14
Unknown Infant, no Age, 16
Unknown Infant, no Age, 16
Unknown no Age, 17
Unknown Infant, 3 hours, 18
Unknown Infant, no Age, 18
Unknown no Age, found Dead, 19
Unknown Infant, 5 months, 19
Unknown, 27
Unknown Infant, no age, 35

Valentine Eva, 10
Valentine Martha A, 11
Venable Rebecca, 14
Vaughn Mary, Infant of, 17

Venable Mattie, Infant of, 20
Venable Elvira, 25

Wilkinson Susan, 1
Wooldridge W^m R, 1
Washington Parthemia, 1
Walker Cynthy, 2
Winfree John S, 2
Watkins Sallie, 2
Walker Margret E, 3
Whitmore Jno, Infant of, 3
Washington George, 3
Washington Jno, Thomas, 3
White Jacob, 4
Watkins Julia, 4
Watkins Francis W, 4
Wooldradge Richard M, 4
Wilkinson Daniel, Infant of, 4
Watkins Betty, 5
Worsham Thos, B, 5
White James T, 5
Wooldradge Maurace, 5
Wiley Geo, 5
Woodson Elanora, 6
Walker Patsey, 6
Williams James, 6
Woodson Spencer, 6
White Lucy, 7
Worsham William C, 7
White Ed^{wd}, Infant of, 7
Wallace William E, 7
Wooldridge Richard I, 7
Wathall Woodson, 7
Williams Elizabeth, 8
White Ann, 8
Walker Joseph, 8
Whitlock H, H, 9

Williams Bettie, Infant of, 9
Willboe Clarence, 9
Wilkinson Daniel, 10
Wilkinson Mattie, Infant of, 10
Wiley Bertie, 10
Winfree Rebecca, 10
Watkins Peter, 11
Winfree Fanny, 11
Ward Mary, 11
White Amelia, Infant of, 12
Winfree Ida, 12
Wooldridge Richard, 12
Wright Colan, 12
Wirt Nannie, 13
White Amey, 13
Wodridge Samuel, 13
White John, 13
Winfree Estelle, 13
West Catherine, 14
Warren W^m, 15
Wright Jack, Infant of, 15
Williams Bessie May, 15
Williams Cord, 15
Wooten Ella, 16
White Sam, 16
Whitteker Jessee, 17
Watson Richard, 18
Wright Alsey, 18
Wingfield Florence, 19
Wooldridge Jas, C, 20
Wells Lewis, 20
Williams Belle, 20
Walker Lucinda, 21
Washington Delphia, 22
Williams Ruth, 24,
Williams Susan, 24

Williams Jno, & Wife, Infant of, 24
Walke Thos, 25
Woody Isam, 25
Washington Betsy Ann, 25
Winston Bansey, 25
Wiley Aubrey, 25
Wrenn Joshua, 25
Woolridge Cornelius, 26
West Jno, P, 26
Waddell Ira, 27
Wilder Lucile A, 28
Washington Howard Lee, 28
Washington Wilhart, 29
West Adelia, 29
Wathall Chas, H, 30
White Charlotte, 30
Willson Emma, 33
Williams Clara, 33
Wiley Sallie, 33
Worsham Margarett, 34
Whitehead John, 35
Walker W, & Wife, Infant of, 35
Williams Tom, 35
Winfree W^m, 36
Winston Willie, 36
Watson Arthur, 36
Williams Martha, 37
Wyatt Mathews, 37
Winston Edwd, 37
Waddele Clara, 38
White Leroy, 38
Williams Lethia, 39
Winfree Charlotte, 39
Washington Robert, 39
Waller C, L, 40
White Sallie, 40

Woolridge Martha, 41

Young Elizabeth, 16
Young Anna Bell, 23
Young Elizabeth, 34

INTERMENT ENTRIES

[Editorial note for the following transcription: The original register page numbers are listed in brackets before the entries that appeared on the respective pages. To aid with date tracking, the year has been added to the top of each transcription page.]

[Page 1]

<u>1875</u>

Jul 1; **Susan Dixon**; number 7.

Jul 12; **Elija Miller**; 11m; number 8. [Front index lists as "Eliza Miller."]

Jul 31; **Infant** [NBN: "Entered as Unknown"]; unknown [cause of death]; number 9; found in a field in Manchester.

Aug 29; **Susan Wilkinson**; 90y; widow; old age; div 1; cir 3; sec 68.

Sep 1; **Ellen Mingleton**; 17y; female; single; div 1; cir 3; sec 68.

Sep 4; **Eddie Nelson Morris**; 10m 8d; male; div 1.

Sep 10; **Emily Davies**; 1y 1m; female; div 1; circle 3; sec 66.

Sep 12; **Bessie Fleming**; 3y; female; div 1; sec 64.

Sep 26; **Elisabeth Baugh**; 60y; female; married; debility; div 1; circle 3; sec 54.

Oct 2; **Jackson Jones**; 5m; male; number 10.

Oct 13; **Mary E. Clark**; 8y 1m 3d; female; div 8; sec 1.

Dec 4; **Mary Bell**; 2y; female; number 11.

1876

Mar 16; **Richard Ridley**; 24y; male; married; injured on railroad; brakeman; div 2; number 1.

Mar 21; **Parthemia Burwell**; 75y; female; widow; old age; div 8; sec 2.

Mar 21; **Anderson Burwell**; 60y; male; married; div 8; sec 2. removed from Manchester.

Mar 29; **Wm R. Wooldridge**; 3y 1m; male; croup; div 8; sec 4.

Apr 11; **Armstead Jones**; 53y; male; married; congestion of lungs; laborer; div 8; sec 5.

Apr 17; **Joshua Jeser**; 22y; male; single; consumption; tobacco factory hand; number 12. [Front index lists as "Joshua Jeter."]

May 5; **Nancy Clark**; 60y; female; single; spinal meningitis; number 13.

Jul 10; **Beverly Robinson**; 40y; male; married; sun stroke; factory hand.

Jul 13; **Lelia Moore**; 1y 6m 12d; female; convulsions; div 8; sec 3.

Jul 14; **Annie Turner**; 2y; female; unknown [cause of death]; number 14.

Aug 19; **Emma Morris**; 4m; female; number 15.

Sep 5; **Elizabeth Baugh**; 6m; female; convulsions; cir 3; sec 54.

Oct 4; **Infant of Jas Goode**; male; still born; div 8; sec 4.

[1876 cont.]

Oct 10; **Robt Carter**; 57y; male; div 8; sec 2; removed from Chesterfield County.

Oct 10; **Parthemia Washington**; 27y; female; div 8; sec 2; removed from Chesterfield County.

Oct 10; **Abner Dean**; 3y 1m 7d; male; div 8; sec 2; removed from Chesterfield County.

Oct 16; **Henry Jackson**; 4y 3m; male; diarrhera; div P. D. 22; number 16; removed from Manchester.

Oct 16; **Robert Smith**; male; div 17; sec 2; removed from Manchester.

Oct 16; **Louisa Poindexter**; female; div 17; sec 2; removed from Manchester.

[Page 2]

Oct 16; **Annie Mayo**; female; div 17; sec 2; removed from Manchester.

Oct 16; **William Mayo**; male; div 17; sec 2; removed from Manchester.

Oct 16; **Patsey Brooks**; female; div 17; sec 2; removed from Manchester.

Oct 16; **Nancy Clarke**; female; div 17; sec 2; removed from Manchester.

Oct 16; **George E Mayo**; male; div 17; sec 2; removed from Manchester.

Richmond, Virginia, Mt. Olivet Cemetery Register

[1876 cont.]

Oct 16; **Arromento Mayo**; male; div 17; sec 2; removed from Manchester.

Oct 16; **William R Mayo**; male; div 17; sec 2; removed from Manchester.

Nov 24; **John Henry Holmes**; 8d; male; convulsions; div 2; number 2.

Dec 2; **Wilson Allen**; 58y; male; old age; div PD 22; number 17.

Dec 5; **Infant**; [NBN: "Entered as unknown."] female; from drowning; div PD 22; number 9½.

Dec 6; **Thomas Burk**; 85y; male; married; from old age; laborer; div PD 22; number 18.

Dec 7; **James Anderson**; 35y; male; married; epilepsy; laborer; div PD 22; number 19.

Dec 10; **Sarah Jane Anderson**; 5m; female; pnuemonia; div PD 22; number 19.

Dec 18; **Mariah** [NBN: "Entered as Mariah under M's"]; female; old age; div PD 22; number 20.

Dec 19; **Tandy Morriss**; 73y; male; married; apoplexy; laborer; div 2; number 3.

1877

Jan 15; **Lizzie Burfoot**; 24y; female; married; consumption; nurse; div 2; number 4.

Jan 16; **Cynthy Walker**; 17y; female; single; consumption; div 2; number 6.

Richmond, Virginia, Mt. Olivet Cemetery Register

[1877 cont.]

Jan 20; **John Jonathan**; 70y; widower; pneumonia; laborer; div 1; cir 1; sec 18.

Feb 7; **Julia Stronn**; 8y; female; debility; div PD 22; number 21.

Feb 19; **Infant of Thomas Hix**; div PD 22; number 22.

Mar 25; **Florence C. Burfoot**; 10m; female; pneumonia; div 2; number 5.

Mar 25; **John Banks**; 50y; male; married; rail road accident; fireman; div 2; number 7.

Apr 12; **Infant of Bettie Cole**; still borne; div 22; number 23.

Apr 18; **Celia Ackerman**; 29y; perelmittis [?]; div 2; number 8; died in New York.

May 10; **Child of Hanna Mathews**; still borne; div PD 22.

Jun 4; **Elizabeth Robins**; 22y; female; married; congestion of lungs; div 8; sec 3.

Jun 21; **Aaron Swoon**; 40y; male; drowning; div PD 22.

Jul 4; **Infant of Delia Smith**; 3d; female; suffocation; div PD 22. ["Unknown" interred in same grave on Feb 17, 1879.]

Jul 21; **Jennie Howlett**; female; old age; div PD 22.

Aug 13; **Walter Randolph**; 7y 8m; male; typhoid fever; div 2; number 9.

Aug 25; **Josephine Haxall**; 48y; female; married; dropsey; div 2; number 10.

Richmond, Virginia, Mt. Olivet Cemetery Register

[1877 cont.]

Aug 30; **Unknown**; 12y; male; drowning; div PD 22.

Sep 11; **Sarah Lewis**; 68y; widow; cancer; div 8; sec 2.

Sep 11; **Willie Stewart**; 3y; male; natural cause; div PD 22.

Oct 4; **Henry Randolph**; 35y; male; consumption; div 2; number 11.

Oct 4; **Mary Johnson**; 3y; female; fever; div 16.

Oct 25; **Martha Jackson**; female; softening of brain; div PD 22.

Nov 16; **Anica Cheatham**; 60y; female; widow; dropsy; div PD 22.

Nov 17; **Genevive Hughes**; 2y 1m 10d; female; brain disease; div 17; sec 3.

Nov 18; **John S Winfree**; 5m; male; pneumonia; div 2; number 12.

Dec 23; **Caroline King**; 90y; widow; old age; nurse; div 2; number 13.

Dec 24; **Adam Moore**; 55y; male; single; excessive drink; lab[r]; div 22.

Dec 26; **Sallie Watkins**; 68y; female; div 22.

1878

Jan 7; **Mary E Randolph**; 36y; married; consumption; div 17; sec 3.

Jan 7; **Ann Coleman**; 30y; married; heart disease; cook; div 22.

Richmond, Virginia, Mt. Olivet Cemetery Register

[1878 cont.]

Jan 14; **Willie Flemming**; 3y 3m; male; diptheria; div 1; cir 3; sec 64.

Jan 22; **Lizzie Hicks**; 40y; married; consumption; div 22.

[Page 3]

Feb 2; **Infant of Ellen Harris**; female; still born; div 22.

Feb 19; **Charlott Guthrie**; 32y; married; consumption; div 1; cir 1; sec 18.

Feb 25; **Cornelia Bland**; 4y; female; diptheria; div 2; number 14.

Feb 27; **Mary Ellen Mayo**; 8m; div 17; sec 2.

[Note: the register skips from Feb 27, 1878 to May 20, 1878.]

[The Appendix contains the Manchester Mayor's March 15, 1878 speech to the Manchester City Council as written in the minutes. Note his discussion regarding cemetery sections not being marked which "might lead to great confusion."]

May 20; **Rebecca Jackson**; 2y 11m; female; div 17; sec 1.

Jun 28; **Infant of Wm Smith**; female; still born; div 22.

Jul 22; **John Jackson**; 4m 2d; male; congestion of brain; div 17; sec 1.

Jul 23; **Florence A Cunningham**; 3y 6m 5d; female; brain fever; div 1; cir 1; sec 18.

Jul 31; **Julia Ann Johnson**; 8m 29d; female; congestion brain; div 2; number 15.

Richmond, Virginia, Mt. Olivet Cemetery Register

[1878 cont.]

Aug 6; **Margaret E Walker**; 6y; female; congestion of brain; div 2; number 16.

Aug 7; **Julia Goode**; 40y; female; married; consumption; div 8; sec 3.

Aug 26; **Infant of John Whitmon**; still born; div 8; sec 3. [Front index lists as "Infant of John Whitmore."]

Sep 8; **Infant of Mary Taylor**; still born; div 22.

Oct 1; **Willie Adkins**; 3m; male; div 1; cir 1; sec 18.

Oct 28; **Jordan Goff**; 70y; male; div 2; number 17; died in Chesterfield Co.

Nov 1; **Bernard Keyley**; 2m; male; murusmus; div 8; sec 5.

Nov 21; **Mary Smith**; 10y; female; single; typhoid fever; div 2; number 18.

Dec 21; **Mary Jane Finey**; 26y; married; unknown [cause of death]; div 8; sec 3.

Dec 30; **James R Monroe**; 49y; widower; consumption; barber; div 22.

1879

Jan 3; **Jane Mayo**; 35y; female; div 8, sec 3.

Jan 8; **James Trent**; 54y; male; div 2; number 19.

Feb 4; **Jane Claiborne**; 51y; female; cancer; div 2; number 20.

[1879 cont.]

Feb 14; **Walter Mingleton**; 23y 1m 12d; male; consumption; div 1; cir 3; sec 68.

Feb 17; **Unknown**; female; found dead; div 22; in grave with Delia Smith's child. [Infant of Delia Smith interred on Jul 4, 1877.]

Feb 20; **Infant of Bertha Smith**; 21d; male; convulsions; div 22; in grave with George Washington. [George Washington interred on Feb 24, 1879.]

Feb 24; **George Washington**; male; natural cause; div 22. [Infant of Bertha Smith interred on Feb 20, 1879.]

Mar 31; **Welthy Jane Baker**; 1m 10d; female; pneumonia; div 2; number 21.

May 1; **Jennie Harriss**; 80y; female; married; old age; div 2; number 22.

May 11; **Robert Johnson**; 62y; male; dropsey; div 2; number 23.

May 18; **Matilda Bolling**; 73y; widow; apoplexy; div 2; number 24.

May 30; **Ja^s Taylor**; 59y; married; consumption; div 1; cir 3; sec 68. [Jno Thomas Washington interred on Jun 13, 1879.]

Jun 9; **Jacob Carter**; 72y; male; married; old age; div 8; sec 2.

Jun 13; **Jno Thomas Washington**; 3y; male; consumption; div 1; cir 3; sec 68; in grave with James Taylor. [James Taylor interred on May 30, 1879.]

Jul 3; **Ida Jane Hughes**; 7m 6d; female; cholera infantum; div 17; sec 3.

[1879 cont.]

Jul 5; **Walter Christian**; male; unknown [cause of death]; div 22; died at City Jail Manchester.

Jul 9; **Taylor King**; 1y; male; div 22.

Jul 14; **Child of C. M. Hendley**; 1y; female; unknown [cause of death]; div 1, cir 3; sec 68; in grave with Susan Wilkinson. [Susan Wilkinson interred on Aug 29, 1875.]

Jul 30; **Joseph Booker**; 64y; male; apoplexy; div 2; number 25; died in Chesterfield.

Sep 2; **Ellen Joseph Jefferson**; 1y 3m; female; brain fever; div 22.

Sep 16; **Victoria Miller**; 35y; female; convulsions; div 17; sec 6.

Sep 19; **Eliza Lives**; 55y; widow; apoplexy; div 8; sec 1.

Sep 27; **Robt Mosby**; 60y; male; married; natural causes; div 22.

Nov 9; **Wilson Randolph**; 70y; male; married; paralysis; div 17; sec 3.

Nov 29; **George Revely**; male; div 22.

Dec 1; **Mary E. Baker**; 1y 6m; female; desease of kidney; div 17; sec. 5.

Dec 17; **Amy Cheatham**; 40y; female; peritonitis; div 22.

[Page 4]

Dec 22; **Grant Johnson**; 11y; male; inflamation of bowls; div 22.

Dec 29; **Richard Johnson**; 5y; male; div 22.

Richmond, Virginia, Mt. Olivet Cemetery Register

[Note: the register skips from Dec 29, 1879 to Mar 8, 1880.]

1880

Mar 8; **Julia Baugh**; 9m; female; diptheria; div 1; cir 3, sec 54.

Mar 10; **Infant**; female; still born; div 22.

Mar 11; **Jacob White**; male; married; desiase of heart; div 2; number 26.

Apr 7; **Julia Watkins**; 37y; female; married; convulsions; div 2; number 27. [Francis W. Watkins interred in same grave on Jun 30, 1880.]

Apr 16; **Joe Cox**; 48y; male; softening of brain; div 17; sec 4.

Apr 24; **Infant of Eliza Boyd**; 18d; male; lockjaw; div 22.

Apr 30; **James Brown**; 10y; male; hemmorrhage; div 22.

May 13; **Lewis Randolph**; 13[?]y 8d; male; heart disease; div 22.

Jun 24; **Thomas Potts**; 65y; male; married; pneumonia; div 2; number 28.

Jun 30; **Francis W. Watkins**; 8m; male; brain fever; div 2; number 27; in grave with Julia Watkins. [Julia Watkins interred on Apr 7, 1880.]

Jul 7; **Wm Smith**; 2m; male; measles; div 1; cir 3; cir sec 54. [Leray Smith interred in same grave on Jul 24, 1880.]

Jul 24; **Leray Smith**; 1y 11m; male; hooping cough; div 1; cir 3, sec 54; in grave with Wm Smith. [Wm Smith interred on Jul 7, 1880.]

Richmond, Virginia, Mt. Olivet Cemetery Register

[1880 cont.]

Jul 30; **Susan Coleman**; 37y; female; married; peritonatis [?]; div 22.

Aug 2; **Czar Graves**; 1y; male; asthma; div 17; sec 5.

Sep 22; **Nancy Mann**; 45y; married; womb disease; div 2; number 29.

[Note: the register skips from September 22, 1880 to November 1880.]

Nov 23; **Stephen Baugh**; 76y; widower; wheelwright ocupation; div 1; cir 3; sec 54.

Nov 27; **James Smith**; 5m; male; convulsions; div 22.

Dec 16; **Mary Saunders**; 6m; female; cold & want; div 22.

Dec 22; **Edie Ross**; 50y; female; single; poverty; div 22.

1881

Jan 11; **Wesley Garrate**; 38y; male; killed on RR; fireman; div 2; number 30.

Jan 15; **Infant of Sarah Haxell**; 2y 6m; female; unknown [cause of death]; div 22.

Feb 7; **Richard M. Wooldradge**; 7m; male; unknown [cause of death]; div 8; sec 4.

Mar 7; **Lewis Reade**; 29y; male; congestive fever; div 2; number 31.

Mar 27; **Edmund Turpin**; 30y; male; hemorage; div 8; sec 3.

[1881 cont.]

Apr 4; **Ellen Hill**; 30y; female; married; uterian disease; div 2; number 32.

Apr 9; **Anna Bell Green**; 25y; female; child birth; div 22.

May 27; **Frank Sydnor**; 60y; male; malarial fever; div 22.

May --; **Ballard T. Edwards**; 52y 5m 17d; male; married; softening of brain; div 17; part of sec ½ 5.

Jun 22; **Henry Bland** [NBN: "Entered as Bland"); 2m; male; cholera infantum; div 1; cir 3, sec 54.

Jun 27; **Infant of Mariah Keeling**; 2y; female; div 8; sec 5.

Jul 18; **Mary Flemming**; 60y; female; natural cause; div 22.

Aug 14; **Eva Goode**; 70y; female; dropsy; div 22. [Infant of Alice Taylor interred in same grave on Aug 14, 1881.]

Aug 14; **Infant of Alice Taylor**; 1y 3m; female; diarrhoea; div 22; in grave with Eva Goode. [Eva Goode interred on Aug 14, 1881.]

Aug 18; **Boyd** [apparently listed as last name]; consumption; div 22.

Sep 19; **Martha Banks**; 80y; widow; dropsy; div 1; cir 1; sec 18.

Oct 2; **Paulina Giles**; 65y; widow; congestion of liver; div 17; sec 6.

Oct 18; **Infant of Daniel Wilkinson**; 8d; female; div 1; cir 3; sec 68.

Dec 10; **Alex Giles**; 27y; single; consumption; div 2; number 33.

Richmond, Virginia, Mt. Olivet Cemetery Register

[1881 cont.]

Dec 24; **Rebecca Morton**; 55y; married; div 2; number 34.

1882

Jan 28; **Infant of Jno Rollins**; convulsions; div 22.

Feb --; **Ceasar Graves**; 40y; married; congestion of lungs; div 17; sec 5.

Jul 5; **Douglass Baugh**; 1y 7m; male; cholera infantum; div 1; cir 3; sec 54.

[Page 5]

Jul 19; **Indianna Johnson**; 44y; widow; div 1; cir 1; sec 18.

Aug 9; **Lewis Fleming**; 30y; married; heart disease; div 2; number 35.

Aug 30; **Lucy Taylor**; 28y; married; consumption; div 8; sec 5.

Aug 31; **Archer Morris**; div 22.

Sep 8; **Judy Jones**; 71y; widow; diarrhoea; div 8; sec 1.

Sep 15; **No name listed**; 18y; female; typ[hoid] fever; div 22.

Sep 27; **Eliza Jones**; 30y; female; consumption; div 22.

Oct 1; **Mary Hays**; 75y; widow; old age; div 2; number 36.

Oct 2; **Chas Lovelace**; 30y; male; congestion fever; div 22.

Oct 14; **Infant of Hattie Heath**; div 22.

Oct 25; **Julia Jenkins**; 18y; consumption; div 1; cir 1; sec 18.

[1882 cont.]

Nov 2; **Betty Watkins**; 26y; consumption; div 8; sec 5.

Dec 23; **Roderick Chandler**; 38y; male; single; congestion of lungs; div 2; number 37.

1883

Jan 30; **Charles Jones**; 12y; male; hooping cough; div 8; sec 5.

May 6; **Francis Thompson**; 27y; single; spinal disease; div 8; sec 4.

May --; **Inf of John Rawlings**; premature birth; div 22.

Jun 3; **Lucie M Brooks**; 1y 9m; female; consumption; div 17; sec 7.

Jul 1; **Thos. B. Worsham**; 20y 10m; male; hemorage; div 8; sec 3.

Jul 24; **Emily Robinson**; 9m; female; typho malarial; div 17; sec 4.

[Note: the register skips from July 24, 1883 to October 11, 1883]

Oct 11; **Pearl A Johnson**; 3y 5m 2d; female; marasmus; div 8; sec 4.

Nov 28; **Archer Dennis**; 100y; div 22.

Dec 9; **Mrs Mary Brooks**; 34y; married; consumption; div 17; sec 7.

Dec 25; **Jas Coleman**; 45y; married; asthma; div 22.

Dec 26; **Wm Smith**; 60y; single; consumption; div 22.

1884

Jan 4; **James T White**; 39y; single; heart disease; div 22.

Jan 7; **Maurace Wooldradge**; 30y; married; dropsy; div 8; sec 4.

Feb 14; **Geo Wiley**; 23y; single; congestion of lungs; div 2, number 39.

[Entered after Geo Wiley in between lines:] (Townsend)

Mar 1; **Thos Gibson**; 60y; married; typho mal [?] fev; div 17; sec 1.

Mar 11; **Alberta Smith**; 3y; female; dypthirea [?]; div 1; cir 3; sec 54.

Mar 14; **Mary Burfoot**; 75y; married; rhumatism; div 17; sec 4.

Mar 16; **Willis Powell**; 7d; male; convulsions; div 1; cir 1; sec 18.

Apr 16; **Rachael Randolph**; 70y; married; inflammation of brain; div 17; sec 3.

Apr 20; **Emma Lawson**; 23y; consumption; div 2; number 40.

May 3; **Jos Dickenson**; 13y; single; dropsey; div 17; sec 6. [Front index lists as "Jos Dickerson."]

May 26; **William E Mayo**; 6m; male; pneumonia; div 17; sec 2.

Jul 6; **Isham Jenkins**; 69y; widower; appoplexy; div 2; number 41.

Jul 9; **Elizabeth Baugh**; 7m; congestion of lungs; div 1; cir 3; sec 54.

Jul 22; **Martha Baker**; married; consumption; div 2; number 42.

[1884 cont.]

Aug 3; **Mary E Gains**; 2y 11m; acute diarrhoea; div 2; number 43.

Aug 28; **Andrew Love**; 2y; teething; div 22.

Sep 1; **Infant Keyo**; 5m; female; congestion; div 17; sec 6.

Sep 2; **Sally Armsted**; 70y; widow; paralysis; div 2; number 44.

[Page 6]

Oct 4; **Elizabeth Harriss**; 71y; widow; none of late [in disease column]; div 2; number 45.

Oct 14; **L H Barcroff**; 8m; male; congestion of brain; div 8.

Oct 16; **Ama Tatum**; 19y; female; unknown [cause of death]; div 22.

Oct 21; **Harvey OBland**; 3m 12d; male; dysentary; div 1; cir 1; sec 18.

Oct 22; **Kate Dandridge**; 25y; married; consumption; div 1; cir 3; sec 54.

Nov 26; **Alexander Briggs**; 48y; married; heart disease; div 17; sec 3.

Dec 6; **Sarah Baugh**; 9m; infantile diarrhoea; div 1; cir 3; sec 54.

1885

Jan 6; **Margaret E Johnson**; 33y; married; consumption; div 8; sec 1.

[1885 cont.]

Jan 30; **Andrew Smith**; 28y; married; consumption; div 1; cir 3; sec 1.

Jan 30; **Robt Smith**; 5m; typho fever; div 1; cir 3; sec 1.

Feb 16; **Elanora Woodson**; 5y 10m; typho pneumonia; div 1; cir 3; sec 68.

Mar 27; **Charles Mann**; 31y; married; div 2; number 46.

Apr 3; **Infant of Wanda Booker**; div 22.

Apr 7; **Mildred Baugh**; 3m; female; congestion of liv[er]; div 1; cir 3; sec 54.

Jun 1; **Adeline Harris**; 17y; single; phthisis; div 2; number 47.

Jun 11; **Mat Burfoot**; 72y; married; old age; div 17; sec 4.

Jun 22; **Edward Davis**; 1y 6m; congestion of brain; div 22.

Jul 21; **Unknown Infant**; congestion of lungs; div 22.

Aug 6; **Mary Hewlett**; 1y 2m; congestion of lungs; div 1; cir 3; sec 68.

Aug 12; **Nannie Johnston**; div 22.

Aug 13; **Rhoda Goode**; 13y; accidental burning; div 22.

Sep 6; **Alice Taylor**; 32y; unknown [cause of death]; div 22.

Sep 9; **Clarence Paine**; 1y 6m; marasmus; div 22.

Sep 18; **Patsey Walker**; 53y; married; consumption; div 8; sec 1.

Richmond, Virginia, Mt. Olivet Cemetery Register

[1885 cont.]

Sep 19; **James W. Blackwell**; 55y; married; inflamation; div 17; sec 1.

Sep 20; **Ruth Johnson**; 1y 14d; congestion of lungs; div 8; sec 1.

Oct 1; **Infant** [NBN: "Entered as unknown"]; 21d; male; marasmus; div 1; cir 3; sec 1.

Oct 16; **Julia Johnson**; 50y; widow; cancer of stomach; div 22.

Nov 18; **Clara Robinson**; 45y; widow; dropsey; div 17; sec 1.

1886

Jan 20; **Edward Dean**; 67y; appoplexy; div 8; sec 2.

Jan 20; **W. R. Randolph**; 50y; chronic; div 17; sec 3.

Jan 27; **Ella W Burfurd**; 17y; single; consumption; div 2; number 48.

Jan 27; **Bessie Hughes**; 5m 4d; spasums; div 17; sec 3.

Mar 3; **Blanche Thompson**; 1m 5d; convulsions; div 1; cir 1; sec 18.

Mar 13; **Mary Saunders**; 80y; widow; gangrene; div 2; sec 49.

Mar 29; **Lucy A Hall**; 69y; married; paralysis of heart; div 2; number 50.

Apr 19; **Lucy Cassell**; 65y; widow; paralysis of heart; div 22.

Jun 8; **Susan E Johnson**; 12y 3m; typho fever; div 2; number 51.

Jun 10; **Infant** [NBN: "Entered under unknown"]; div 22.

[1886 cont.]

Jul 22; **Coleman Harris**; 5m; diarrhoea; div 1; cir 3; sec 68.

Aug 12; **James Williams**; 46y; div 1; cir 3; sec 54.

Aug 25; **Elizabeth Robertson**; 90y; widow; old age; div 17; sec 4.

Sep 4; **Geo Taylor**; 34y; married; heart disease; div 2.

Sep 8; **Jennie Holmes**; 45y; widow; malarial fever; div 1; cir 3; sec 68.

Sep 12; **Mary Smith**; 1y 2m 10d; malarial fever; div 1; cir 3; sec 54.

Oct 3; **Spencer Woodson**; 38y; married; consumption; div 1; cir 3; sec 68.

[Page 7]

Oct 4; **James Robinson**; 23y; single; killed on R. R.; div 2; number 53.

Oct 15; **Charles Thompson**; 74y; married; congestion of kidneys; div 2; number 54.

Oct 20; **Lucy White**; 20y; single; div 22.

Oct 24; **Mary Edwards**; 10y; consumption; div 1; cir 3; sec 68.

Oct 25; **Eugine Henderson**; 3y; croup; div 2; number 55.

Oct 25; **Carter G DeJusto**; 2y 6m 19d; congestion of lungs; div 2; number 56.

Oct 26; **Priscilla Robertson**; 38y; consumption; div 8; sec 1.

Richmond, Virginia, Mt. Olivet Cemetery Register

[1886 cont.]

Nov 18; **Eliza Carter**; 21y; single; dropsey; div 22.

Dec 20; **Willie Booker**; 10y; single; consumption; div 8; sec 1.

Dec 21; **Antelia Finney**; 12y; female; consumption; div 1; cir 3; sec 68.

1887

Jan 2; **Mary Ellen Bailey** [NBN: "Entered as Bailey"]; 15m; female; membranvus croup; div 1; cir 3; sec 68.

Jan 9; **Milley Dickerson**; 36y; female; cancer of womb; div 17; cir 2; sec 6.

Jan 21; **Albert Jones**; 40y; married; paralysis; laborer; div 8; sec 4.

Feb 10; **Infant of Rebecca Thomas**; still born; div 22.

Feb 13; **William C Worsham**; 23y; male; consumption; div 2 number 57; brought from Baltimore.

Feb 14; **Abbey Hudlett**; 30y; single; spinal & heart disease; div 17; sec 4 [?].

Feb 17; **Infant of Ed^{wd} White**; 10d; female; not mentioned [cause of death]; div 22.

Mar 1; **No Name** [NBN: "Entered as unknown"]; male; still born; div 22.

Mar 14; **George Hewlett**; 30y; single; drowned; div 22.

Apr 2; **No Name** [NBN: "Entered as unknown"]; still born; div 22.

Richmond, Virginia, Mt. Olivet Cemetery Register

[1887 cont.]

Apr 17; **Rachael Allen**; 4m; female; pertussis & complications; div 2; number 58.

May 2; **Henry Robinson**; male; killed by carrs; div 17; sec 1 [?].

May 2; **Christian** [apparently listed as last name]; male; div 22; number 62.

May 30; **L. J. Meeborn**; 24m; male; consumption; div 2; number 59.

Jun 10; **Giles Miller**; 56y; widower; anasaica [?] from cardiac; div 17; sec 6.

Jun 21; **Ruth Thomas**; 1m; female; dysentery & convulsions; div 1; cir 1; sec 18.

Jun 23; **Carrie Burford**; 7m; female; measles; div 17; sec 4.

Jul 4; **William E Wallace**; 48y; married; abcess of brain; div 22; number 63; brought from central lunatic asylum.

Jul 15; **Eva B. Hall**; 1y 1m; female; diarrhoea; div 2; number 60.

Jul 25; **Stephen Keys**; 13y; male; accidental drownding; div 17; sec 6.

Jul 27; **Bettie Hunt**; 29y; married; dysentery; div 2; number 61.

Jul 31; **Maria Burke**; 53y; married; paralysis; div 2; number 62.

Aug 12; **Lucy Ambler**; 50y; married; typhoid fever; div 22; sec 64.

Aug 21; **Viola Coy**; 8y; single; inflammation bowels; div 8; sec 4.

Richmond, Virginia, Mt. Olivet Cemetery Register

[1887 cont.]

Aug 25; **Infant of Liddia Ruffin**; still born; div 22; number 64.

Sep 6; **Nancy Johnson**; 54y; widow; general dropsy; div 2; number 63.

Sep 13; **Richard I. Wooldridge**; 11m; male; diarrhoe; div 8; sec 4.

Sep 14; **Malinda Davis**; 36y; female; tubercolis; div 22; number 65.

Sep 20; **Unknown Infant**; drowned in well; div 22; number 65.

Sep 25; **Ella Morrison**; 19y 8m 23d; married; typhoid fever; div 2; number 64.

Sep 27; **Stephen Barbell**; 75y; single; old age & ulcerated leg; div 22; number 66. [Front index lists as "Stephen Barbelt."]

Sep 30; **Woodson Walthall**; 35y; married; consumption; div 1; cir 3; sec 64.

[Page 8]

Oct 20; **Elizabeth Williams**; 10y; single; dyptheria croup; div 15; sec 54.

Oct 23; **Henry Dandridge**; 30y; married; consumption; black smith; div 1; cir 1.

Dec 14; **Hilton Brooks Jr.**; 3y; single; typhoid fever; div 2; number 65.

Dec 16; **Charlie Twine**; 18y; single; consumption; div 2; number 66.

[1887 cont.]

Dec 16; **Eliza Lipscomb**; 59y; married; cronic inflam of liver; div 2; number 69.

Dec 18; **Loula A. Henderson**; 15y 6m; single; tubercalosis; div 2; number 67.

Dec 26; **Pashal Robinson**; 39y; married; phthesis peritonuetis[?]; div 2; number 68.

1888

Jan 1; **London Brigge**; 24y; single; consumption; div 2; number 70.

Jan 15; **Isaac Reed**; 75y; widower; consumption & old age; div 22; number 67.

Jan 24; **James Randolph**; 30y; married; softening of brain; div 2; number 71.

Feb 2; **Mary Booker**; 23y; married; consumption; div 2; number 72. [Easter Booker interred in same grave on Jul 25, 1888.]

Feb 9; **Amey Briggs**; 16y; single; dropsy & heart disease; div 2; number 73.

Feb 21; **Daniel Roane**; 50y; married; pneumonia; div 22; number 68.

Feb 26; **Sam'l Meller**; 35y; single; typhoid pneumonia; div 2; number 74.

Feb 27; **Effie S. Green**; 20m; single; diphtheria; div 2; number 75.

Mar 13; **Florence Harris**; 1y 4m; female; died from a burn; div 1; cir 1; sec 19.

[1888 cont.]

Mar 17; **Ethel T. Edwards**; 10d; female; convulsions; div 2; number 76.

Mar 29; **Elvira Peterson**; 40y; widow; heart disease; div 22; number 69.

Mar 31; **Willie Porter**; 18y; single; hemorange of lungs; div 22; number 72.

Apr 1; **Henry Davis**; 6m; male; capillary bronchetis; div 8.

Apr 3; **Cora Stowe** [NBN: "Entered as Stowe"]; 25y; married; heart disease; div 22; number 73.

Apr 5; **Rhoda Binga**; 72y; married; congestion of lungs; div 1; cir 1; sec 20.

Apr 11; **Mary Jackson**; 73y; widow; heart disease; div 17; sec 5.

Apr 19; **Coleman Robinson**; 34y; married, pulmonary consumption; div 2; number 77. [Coleman Robinson's 7 year-old son was interred in same grave on Aug 8, 1890.]

Apr 20; **Amie R. Hilton**; 4y; female; diareha & measles; div 2; number 78.

Apr 20; **Susan A. Jackson**; 23y; married; typhoid fever; div 2; number 78 ½. [Chas Jackson interred in same grave on Jul 16, 1888.]

Apr 28; **Margaret Fitzgerald**; 31y; married; hemorage on abortion; div 2; number 79. [Ella Fitzgerald interred in same grave on Jun 4, 1890.]

Apr 30; **No name** [NBN: "Entered as unknown"]; few hours; female; not given [cause of death]; div 22; number 70.

[1888 cont.]

May 6; **Alice Bailey**; 16y; single; consumption; div 2; number 80.

May 20; **Cora Stowe** [NBN: "Entered as Stowe"]; 4m; female; convulsions; div 22; number 73.

May 30; **Luther Booker**; 3m; male; convulsions; div 22; number 74.

Jun 1; **Elvira Scott**; 77y; married; effects of old age; div 2; number 81. [Mary E. Jackson interred in same grave on May 28, 1890.]

Jun 10; **Ann White**; 19y; single; consumption; div 2; number 82. [James Johnson interred in same grave on Jan 16, 1889.]

Jun 17; **Sarah Robinson**; 31y; married; apoplexy; div 1; cir 3; sec 66.

Jun 17; **Sarah R. Howlett**; 18y; single; consumption; div 2; number 83.

Jun 19; **Lucy Harris**; 82y; female; old age; div 22; number 76.

Jun 20; **Joseph Walker**; 67y; widower; general dibility; div 2; number 84.

Jun 26; **Norma Fowlkes**; 11m; female; marasmus; div 22; number 75.

[Page 9]

Jun 27; **Maggie Tompkins**; 40y; married; consumption; div 1; cir 3; sec 54.

Jun 28; **Mandy Branch**; 8m; female; cholera infantum; div 22; number 77.

Richmond, Virginia, Mt. Olivet Cemetery Register

[1888 cont.]

Jul 1; **Infant of Sallie Hunter**; 14m; female; convulsions; div 22; number 76; two in one grave.

Jul 5; **Charley Hill**; 3m; male; indigestion; div 22; number 78.

Jul 8; **Mollie Baugh**; 4m 7d; female; cholera infantum; div 1; cir 3; sec 54.

Jul 16; **Chas Jackson**; 9m; male; dysentery; in grave with Susan A. Jackson. [Susan A. Jackson interred in same grave on April 20, 1888.]

Jul 17; **J. H. Clay**; 1y 9m; male; dysentery; div 22; number 79.

Jul 25; **Easter Booker**; 1y 6m; female; tubercolis; div 2; number 72; in grave with Mary Booker. [Mary Booker interred on Feb 2, 1888.]

Jul 26; **Blanche Branche**; 7d; female; intero colitis; div 2; number 85.

Jul 31; **Laura A. Thompson**; 4y 10m 30d; female; typhoid dysentery; div 1; cir 1; sec 18.

Aug 19; **Still born children of Magr Turner**; cause not given [cause of death]; div 22; number 80.

Aug 11; **Harry Streets**; 11m 15d; male; inflammation of bowels; div 2; number 88.

Aug 12; **Robert Morton**; 68y; married; tuberculos consumption; div 2; number 86.

Aug 12; **H. H. Whitlock**; 8y 16m; male; marasmus; div 22; number 81.

[1888 cont.]

Aug 19; **Granville Turner**; 15d; male; mennagetis; div 22; number 82.

Aug 18; **Infant of Mary Allen**; 2y; male; not given [cause of death]; div 2; number 87; brought from Chesterfield.

Aug 19; **S. Arthur Coy**; 11m; male; convulsions; div 2; number 89.

Sep 7; **Eddie Branch**; 5m; male; cholera infantum; div 22; number 83.

Sep 11; **Georgie Friend**; 7m; male; cholera infantum; div 22; number 84.

Sep 13; **Susan Gregory**; 100y; female; old age; div 22; number 85.

Sep 14; **Maria Adkins**; 35y; married; fatty degeneration of heart; div 17; sec 5.

Sep 17; **Lewis H. Clarke**; 78y; widower; dysentery; div 2; number 90.

Oct 5; **Still born child of Bettie Williams**; still born; female; premature birth; div 22; number 86.

Oct 18; **John Brooks**; 60y; widower; pneumonia; div 22; number 87.

Oct 18; **Mary M. Baker**; 10y 9m; consumption; div D1; cir 1; sec 22.

Oct 20; **[No name listed]**; [no information listed – not counted in total].

Richmond, Virginia, Mt. Olivet Cemetery Register

[1888 cont.]

Oct 20; **J. H. Fife**; 66y; married; ch" disentery; div 22; number 89.

Oct 23; **Clarence Willbor**; 2y; inanition; div 22; number 90. [Front index lists as "Willboe."]

Oct 29; **Inf of J & M Fountain**; 4m; marasmus; div 22; number 91.

Nov 2; **Marie Southall**; 9m; supposed neglect; div 22; number 92.

Nov 26; **Josephine Logan**; 53y; married; cancer; div D1; cir 1; sec 23.

Dec --; **Eliza I Allen**; 33y; married; phthisis; div D1; cir 1; sec 23.

Dec 11; **Laura Goode**; 29y; single; scirrus [?] of the intereres [?]; div 2; number 91.

Dec 16; **Florence Fife**; 11y; single; diphtheria; div 22; number 93.

Dec 17; **[No Name]**; div 22; number 94; brought from Chesterfield.

Dec 20; **Nancy Banks**; 87y; widow; old age; div 22; number 95.

Dec 18; **Rebeccah Bush**; 73y; widow; softening of brain; div 1; cir 1; sec 20.

Dec 21; **Frances Brown**; 11m; whooping cough; div 2; number 92.

<u>1889</u>

Jan 16; **Hannah Gibson**; 51y; widow; apoplexy; div 17; sec 1.

Jan 30; **Mary H Branch**; 75y; heart disease; div 2; number 93.

[1889 cont.]

Feb 3; **Martha Epps**; 2m 13d; tubercolis; div 2; number 96.

[Page 10]

Feb 12; **George Harris**; 38y; married; heart disease; laborer; div 2; number 94.

Feb 13; **Mary Epps**; 2m; female; valvula trouble; div 22; number 96; two in one grave.

Feb 17; **Child of Sarah Logan**; still born; div 22; number 97.

Mar 11; **Martha Ann Clayborne**; married; mennagetis; div 22; number 98.

Mar 15; **Robert Baker**; 54y; married; pneumonia; div 1; cir 1; sec 24.

Mar 16; **Anna Foster**; 22y; phitersis; div 17; sec 5.

Mar 20; **Burrell Hicks**; 32y; married; perritonitis; div 22; number 99.

Mar 22; **Eva Valentine**; 38y; married; consumption; div 2; number 96. [Martha A. Valentine, her 3-year-old daughter, was interred in same grave on Nov 26, 1889.]

Apr 5; **Florence Howlett**; not given [age]; tubercolis; div 2; number 95.

Apr 4; **Daniel Wilkinson**; 70y; married; valvuear [?] of heart; div 22; number 100.

Apt 11; **Isaac Hall**; 75y; organic [?] of heart; div 2; number 97.

Richmond, Virginia, Mt. Olivet Cemetery Register

[1889 cont.]

Apr 17; **Infant of Mattie Wilkinson**; 2d; premature birth; div 2; number 98.

May 23; **Paulina Burton**; 80y; widow; chrnc diarrhoea; div 2; number 99.

May 26; **Lena E. Edwards**; 4m 25d; female; pneumonia; div 2; number 76; in grave with another child.

Jun 1; **Woodson Branch**; 64y; single; congestion of brain; div 2; number 100.

Jun 7; **Bertie Wiley**; 13y; female; pneumonia; div 2; number 101.

Jun 13; **Merchant Elleott**; 72y; widow; liver disease.

Jun 14; **James E. Ross**; 13y; single; tubercolis of liver & bowels; div 2; number 102. [Chas. A. Ross interred in same grave on Jan 25, 1890.]

Jun 14; **Tom H. Johnson**; 24y; single; consumption; div 1.

Jun 23; **Wm D. Brooks**; 18y 10m 9d; single; consumption; div 7; sec 7.

Jun 26; **Rebecca Winfree**; 4m; female; convulsions; div 2; number 103.

Jul 14; **Welton Clairborne**; 4m; male; cholera infantum; div 22; number 104.

Jul 11; **Lou B. Brown**; 2m; female; cholera infantum; div 2; number 104.

[No date or name]; div 22; number 101.

[1889 cont.]

[No date or name]; div 22; number 102.

Jul 14; **Matte Cabbell**; 14y; female; typhoid fever; div 22; number 103.

Jul 20; **Frank Nelson Sr.**; 81y; dysentery; div 2; number 105.

Jul 23; **Fanny Meckans**; 70y; dysentery; div 22; number 104.

Jul 25; **Addie Moosby**; 15y; female; consumption; div 22; number 105.

Aug 2; **James H. Saunders**; 1y 3m; male; inflammation of bowels; div 2; number 106.

Aug 4; **Anna Christian**; 31y 28d; married; consumption; div 2; number 107.

Aug 14; **Alfred Moosby**; 11m; male; marasmus; div 22; number 107.

Aug 4; **Martha Rudolph**; 3m; male [appears to be gender error]; sudden death; div 22; number 106.

Aug 8; **Albert Baugh**; 3y; male; dropsey; div 1; sec 54.

Aug 18; **William Gray**; 18y 4m 15d; single; phthisis; div 2; number 108.

Aug 22; **Miles Sutherland**; 1y 6m; male; intestinal cataarh [?]; div 2; number 109.

Aug 22; **Matilda Stepheny**; killed by cars; div 2; number 111.

Aug 30; **Joseph Goode**; 52y; married; disease of stomach; div 8; sec 4.

[1889 cont.]

Aug 27; **Nerah Armstead**; 9y; female; typhoid fever; div 2; number 110.

[Page 11]

Sep 8; **Chas Logan**; 15y; male; shotmund [?] & typhoid fever; div 1; cir 1; sec 23.

Sep 24; **Julia Baugh**; 10m; female; dentition; div 1; cir 3; sec 54.

Sep 23; **Richard Simmons**; 39y; married; senticamia {blown up} [sic]; div 2; number 112.

Oct 2; **Samuel Quawls**; 60y; male; organic disease of heart; div 22; number 108.

Oct 12; **Ida Harris**; 2y 6m; female; cholera infantum; div 22; number 109.

Oct 16; **Peter Watkins**; 75y; married; apoplexy; div 22; number 110.

Oct 16; **Amy Morton**; 45y; married; burnt to death; div 22; number 112.

Oct 16; **Bell Peuchaum**; 33y; married; phthisis; div 2; number 113.

Oct 23; **Peter Smith**; 75y; widower; ch. diarrhrea; div 22; number 111.

Oct 29; **Josephine Armstead**; 1y 11m; female; diarrhrea; div 2; number 114.

Nov 4; **Benjiman Foster**; 50y; married; softening of brain.

[1889 cont.]

Nov 6; **Fanny Winfree**; 50y; single; dropsy; div 22; number 113.

Nov 10; **Emanuel Glenford**; 56y; married; rheumatism & dropsey; div 2; number 115.

Nov 22; **Mary Allen**; 25y; married; congestion; div 2; number 116. [Jno. R. Allen interred in same grave on Apr 31, 1890.]

Nov 26; **Martha A. Valentine**; 3y; female; accidental currency[?]; div 2; number 96; in grave with its mother. [Eva Valentine interred on Mar 22, 1889.]

Dec 6; **Fanny Bruce**; 20y; single; consumption; div 22; number 114.

Dec 22; **Rosalia Hill**; 10m 25d; female; dysentery; div 2; number 32; in grave with step mother.

1890

Jan 2; **H. L Henderson**; 14m; convulsions; div 2; number 67; in grave with Lulu Henderson. [Lulu Henderson interred on Dec 18, 1887.]

Jan 16; **James Johnson**; 1y 7m; pneumonia; div 2; number 82; in grave with A. White. [A. White interred on Jun 10, 1888.]

Jan 25; **Chas A. Ross**; 10y; single; consumption; div 2; number 102; in grave with Jas E. Ross. [Jas E. Ross interred on Jun 14, 1889.]

Jan 27; **Isaac Gizzard**; 65y; married; dysentery; div 22; number 115.

Feb 5; **Samuel Allen**; 70y; married; congestion of lungs; div 2; number 117.

[1890 cont.]

Feb 5; **John Coles**; 17y; single; paralysis; div 22; number 116.

Feb 5; **Earnest Cook**; 1m; pneumonia; div 22; number 116; two in one grave.

Feb 9; **Isac Price**; 41y; single; ch. rheumatism & heart disease; div 22; number 117; two in one grave.

Feb 14; **Still-born of Mary Logan**; 0y 0m 0d; female; still born [cause of death]; div 22; number 117.

Feb 20; **Henry Burrell**; 24y; single; consumption; div 22; number 118.

Mar 2; **Infant of Mary Glasgow**; 6d; female; tetanus infantum; div 22; number 119; removed to section 25 div 1.

Mar 3; **Jane Munroe**; 22y; single; puperal fever; div 22; number 120.

Mar 16; **Mollie Glassgow**; 19y; single; congestion of brain; div 1; cir 1; sec 25.

Mar 16; **Alexander Davis**; 34y; married; dropsy; div 1; cir 3; sec 66.

Mar 17; **Thos. Hicks**; 55y; married; dropsy; div 22; number 121.

Mar 21; **Fanny Miller**; 30y; married; dropsy & consumption; div 17; sec 6.

Apr 1; **Mary Ward**; 16y; single; brain fever; div 22; number 122.

Apr 18; **Elishae Bailie**; 40y; married; consumption; div 12; number 118.

60   Richmond, Virginia, Mt. Olivet Cemetery Register

[1890 cont.]

Apr 26; **Annie May Howward**; 10m; congestion of bowels; div 22.

Apr 28; **Rebecca Carmpton**; 25y; single; dysentery; div 22; number 123.

Apr 31; **Mary F. Booker**; 2y 8m; tabes [?] mesenteria; div 8; sec 3; number 124.

Apr 31; **Jno. R Allen**; 7y; typhoid fever; div 2; sec 3; number 116; in grave with mother. [Mary Allen interred on Nov 22, 1889.]

[Page 12]

May 5; **Ocolia Miller**; 18d; female; general debility; div 17; sec 6.

May 15; **Amelia White's child**; still born [age]; still born [cause of death]; div 22; number 124.

May 21; **Wm Henry Rudolph**; 3m; male; ch. infantum; div 22; number 125.

May 22; **Charles & Eliza Thomas**; 4 & 2 yrs; male & female; measles; div 2; number 69; in grave with their mother.

May 26; **Alice P. Thomas**; 6y; female; measles, div 2, number 119.

May 28; **Mary E. Jackson**; 5y 3m; convulscions; div 2; number 81; in grave with Elvira Scott. [Elvira Scott interred on Jun 1, 1888.]

May 30; **Infant Child** [NBN: "Entered as unknown"], 1m 14d; congestion; div 22; number 126.

[1890 cont.]

May 31; **Ida Winfree**; 1 y 3 m; measles & menagetis; div 13; sec 23.

Jun 3; **[No Name]**; div 22; number 127.

Jun 4; **Ella Fitzgerald**; 28d; female; want of vitality; div 2; number 79; in grave with Margarette Fitzgerald. [Margarette Fitzgerald interred on Apr 28, 1888.]

Jun 9; **Lena E. Allen**; 7m 12d; female; not given [cause of death]; div 1; cir 1; sec 26.

Jun 10; **Mary E. Randolph**; 5 weeks; female; convulsions; div 22; number 128.

Jun 16; **Richard Wooldridge**; 58y 3m; married; softening of brain; div 8; sec 4.

Jun 15; **Helen L. Smith**; 2y 5m 9d; epelepesy; div 2; number 103.

Jun 20; **Ella Rollins**; 49y; married; ascelis (cardiac); div 2; number 120.

Jun 25; **Still born of M. & M. Brown**; male; still born [cause of death]; div 2; number 92.

Jun 26; **Emma Robinson**; 3m; female; whooping cough; div 22; number 129.

Jun 26; **Samuel Armstead**; 10m; male; convulsions & teething; div 1; cir 1; sec 27.

Jul 2; **Hattie Coseley**; 1y 5m; female; whooping cough; div 1; cir 1; sec 25.

Jul 13; **Richard Bird**; 25y; single; apoplexy; div 2; number 121.

[1890 cont.]

Jul 16; **John Holmes**; 55y; married; chronic alcholism; div 22; burried in Masonic section.

Jul 21; **Ed Paul Carrington**; 6y; cold & measles; div 22; number 130.

Jul 23; **Al _ _ _ Logan**; 2y; single; consumption; div 2; number 122.

Aug 4; **Emma Jackson**; 38y; married; cardiac rheumatism; div 17; sec 5.

Aug 6; **Betsy Dennis**; 65y; married; gastric fever; div 2; number 123.

Aug 8; **Coleman Robinson**; 7y 10m; male; typhoid fever; div 2; number 77; in grave with father. [Coleman Robinson, Sr. interred on Apr 19, 1888.]

Aug 10; **D. Willie Mayo**; 2y; male; marasmus; div 22; number 131.

Aug 10; **Sam'l Flemming**; married; tubercolis; div 1; cir 3; sec 64.

Aug 17; **Charlie Finney**; 2y 2m; boy; typhoid fever; div 1; cir 1; sec 25.

Aug 19; **Ruth Jackson**; 7m; girl; not given [cause of death]; div 17; sec 5.

Aug 31; **Charles Howell**; 29y; male; angina vestosis; div 2; number 125.

Sep 27; **Henritta Archer**; 60y; female; rhumatism; div 1; cir 1; sec 26.

[1890 cont.]

Oct 9; **Russell Booker**; 7m; male; div 22; number 132.

Oct 5; **Jula Roberson**; 3y 1m; female; malaral fever; div 17; sec 6.

Oct 7; **Abram Narh** [NBN: "Entered under A & N's as Narh Abram & Abram Narh]; 56y; male; dropsy; div 2; number 128.

Oct 22; **Ida C. Erwin**; 26y; female; phthisis pulmonalis; div 1; cir 1; sec 27.

Oct 26; **Colon Wright**; 8y; male; div 2; number 129.

[Page 13]

Nov 23; **Patrick Chapman**; 19y; single; consumption; div 1; cir 1; sec 27.

Nov 23; **Eva Henley**; 9y; female; not stated [cause of death]; div 1; cir 1; sec 22.

Dec 3; **James Price**; 4d; male; marasmus; div 22; number 133.

Dec 8; **Anna Johnson**; 17y; female; consumption; div 22; number 134.

Dec 3; **Chas W. Thomson**; 32y; married; consumption; div 1; cir 1; sec 18.

Dec 9; **Jas Finney**; 35y; haemotysis; div 2; number 130.

Dec 10; **Martha Harris**; 18y 8m 5d; single; pulmonary phthysis; div 2; number 131.

Dec 21; **Estelle Hobson**; 20y; married; pneumonia; div 2; number 132.

Richmond, Virginia, Mt. Olivet Cemetery Register

[1890 cont.]

Dec 23; **Arthur Hews** [number after name: "580"]; 6m; male; croup; div 22; number 135.

[Next line lists "136" in grave number column in error?]

1891

Jan 9; **Cormyton**; 2y; female; marasmus; div 22; number 137.

Jan 12; **Nannie Wirt**; div 22; number 138.

Jan 12; **Lucy I Graham**; 48y; female; phthisis; div 17; sec 10.

Jan 15; **Rosa Mayo**; 1y 6m; female; marasmus; div 22; number 131; two in grave.

Feb 1; **Charles Saunders** [NBN: "Entered as Saunders"]; 40y; male; pneuminea; div 22; number 139.

Feb 1; **Elizabeth Goode**; 60y; female; disiase of heart; div 8; sec 4.

Feb 5; **Roubert Louise** [NBN: "Entered under L's & R's as Louise Roubert & Roubert Louise"]; male; kill by R & Q [?] R. R.; div 2; number 133.

Feb 6; **Perry W. Jones**; 2y; male; tubercola menagetes; div 2; number 134.

Feb 7; **Alice Ball**; 24y; female; dropsy; div 2; number 135.

Feb 9; **Mad Simmon**; 65y; male; phthisis; div 2; number 138.

Feb 14; **Alice Gipson Child no name**; 9d; male; congestion of the loungs; div 22; number 140.

Richmond, Virginia, Mt. Olivet Cemetery Register

[1891 cont.]

Feb 22; **Kizziah Roane**; 65y; married; senile decay; div 2; number 140.

Feb 22; **Wm Gisoni** [NBN: "Entered as Gisoni"]; 18y; male; consumption; div 22; number 141.

Feb 22; **Davis** [apparently listed as last name]; 7m; chronic; div 22; number 143.

Feb 24; **Amy White**; 60y; female; disintery; div 22; number 144.

Mar 6; **Infant of Mary Hudson**; div 22; number 145.

Mar 3; **Samuel Woolridge**; 21y 7m; male; phthisis; div 2; number 141.

Mar 11; **Georgie A. Chandler**; 6m; female; catarrhae; div 22; number 146.

Mar 19; **Doctor Bentley**; 27y; single; consumption; div 2; number 142.

Mar 20; **Susan Harris**; 38y; female; dropsy; div 1; cir 1; sec 25.

Mar 23; **Pittman Robertson**; 61y; male; heart disease; div 2; number 143.

Mar 29; **Thomas Gibson**; 80y; male; artiritis leadreig[?]; div 1; cir 1; sec 29.

Apr 6; **Alice Belle Goode**; 1y 15d; female; pneumonia; div 2; number 136.

Apr 13; **Joh White**; 35y; male; burnt to death; div 22; number 147.

[1891 cont.]

Apr 20; **Joseph Smith**; male; heart disease; div 2; number 144.

Apr 28; **Robert P. R. Randolph**; 5y; male; marasmus; div 2; number 71; two in one grave.

May 4; **Estelle Winfree**; 7m; female; unknown [cause of death]; div 13; sec 23.

May 16; **Infant of M. & S. Robinson**; 0y 0m 0d; male; premature birth; div 2; number 128; two in one grave.

May 21; **Lizzie Randolph**; hydrosephalysis; div 22; number 148.

May 26; **Wm D. Dennis**; 28y; diarrhoea; div 2; number 145.

[Page 14]

Jun 2; **Mat Harris**; 84y; asthma; div 2; number 146.

Jun 6; **Madaline Rieves**; 10m 7d; cholera infantum; div 2; number 48; two in one grave.

Jun 3; **Mary S. [?] Stokes**; widow; congestion of liver; div 2; number 147.

Jun 21; **Millie Corrington**; 3y; female; marasmus; div 22; number 149.

Jun 23; **Colima** [apparently listed as last name] [NBN: "Entered at Colima"]; 28d; female; dysphrisis [?]; div 22; number 150.

Jun 27; **Patsy Gaines**; 36y; widow; typhoid fever; div 2; number 148.

Jul 14; **Child of Laura Carter**; 3m; female; saofritis [?]; div 22; number 151.

[1891 cont.]

Aug 3; **Joseph H. Carter**; 77y 3m; male; senility; div 1; cir 1; sec 21.

Aug 3; **Thomas Pool**; 28y; male; hepatitis; div 17; sec 5.

Aug 8; **Ananiss Chapman**; 14y; male; typhoid fever; div 1; cir 1; sec 27.

Aug 23; **Fred Hilton**; 70y; male; found in well; div 2; number 149.

Aug 24; **Mariha Marton**; 62y; female; paralysis; div 2; number 150.

Sep 7; **Georgianer Mann**; 22y; female; phthisis; div 1; cir 1; sec 30.

Sep 4; **Martha E. Hilton**; 2y 3m; female; phthisis; number 150.

Sep 5; **James Botts**; 35y; male; chronic diarrhrea; div 22; number 152.

Sep 6; **Garland Thomalson**; 85y; male; old age; div 22; number 153.

Sep 29; **Wm Giles**; 48y; married; inflammation of stomach; div 2; number 151.

Sep 30; **Mrs Fannie Foster**; 38y; widow; pelvis peritonitis.

Oct 28; **Eva Robinson**; 1y 6m 4d; cholera infantum; div 17; sec 6.

Oct 31; **Fanny Flemming**; 85y; old age; div 22; number 154.

Nov 5; **Dolley Hix**; 41y; typhoid fever; div 22; number 156.

68   Richmond, Virginia, Mt. Olivet Cemetery Register

[1891 cont.]

Nov 6; **Edna Bennett**; 1y 8d; peritonitis; div 2; number 152.

Nov 8; **Wm Berryman**; 65; heart disease; div 2; number 153.

Nov 10; **Cyrus Nelson**; 38y; typhoid fever; div 2; number 154.

Nov --; **Catharine West**; 9y; hemorangue; div 22; number 156.

Nov 26; **Aaron Schouren**; 37y; heart disease; div 22; number 157.

Dec 10; **William Irvine**; 5y; la grippe; div 22; number 158.

Dec 18; **Infant of Payton Carter**; 8d; physisis; div 22; number 159.

Dec 18; **Infant of Joseph Goode**; 1/2d; div 2; number 136; two in one grave.

Dec 22; **[No name]**; div 22; number 160.

Dec 26; **Wm Montague**; 10y; single; pneumonia; div 22; number 161.

<u>1892</u>

Jan 25; **Catharine Morton**; 25y; married; phthisis polmonalis; div 2; number 155.

Jan 26; **Susan Johnson**; 26y; single; tubercolis & hemorhangues.

Jan 29; **Jas Robertson**; 2y 1d; male; pneumonia; div 22; number 162.

Feb 1; **Rebecca Venable**; 46y; widow; heart disease; div 2; number 155 ½.

[1892 cont.]

Feb 1; **Francis Armstead**; 24y; single; tubercolis; div 2; number 156.

Feb 5; **No name pauper** [NBN: "Entered under the unknown"]; female; found dead; div 22.

Feb 10; **Lucy Jones**; 10m; female; congestion of lungs; div 1; cir 1; sec 25; two in one grave.

Feb 11; **Wm H. Howard**; 7y; male; pneumonia & grippee; div 2; number 157.

Feb 14; **H. I. Johnson**.

Feb 14; **Augustus Claiborne**; 59y; pneumonia; div 1; cir 1; sec 28.

[Page 15]

Feb 15; **W ^{m} H. Smith**; 37y; married; consumption; buried in Masonic section.

Feb 16; **James Baker**; 63y; married; phthisis; div 2; number 158.

Feb 26; **George Edge**; 2y 4m; shock from burn; div 22; number 163.

Mar 1; **Mary Harris**; 60y; widow; atheroma of cenbive [?]; div 2; number 159.

Mar 2; **Joseph Muse**; 63y; married; rheumatism; div 2; number 160.

Mar 5; **Mary Alia Jasper**; 30y; married; puperil peritonitis; div 2; number 153; in grave with father.

[1892 cont.]

Mar 20; **Sydney Andrews**; 11m; male; convulsions; div 2; number 161.

Mar 20; **Harvey Hayes**; 6m; capilary bronchitis; div 2; number 162.

Mar 17; **Wm Warren**; 50y; widower; heart disease; div 22; number 163.

Mar 22; **Mary Alia Jasper**; 21d; female; acute diarrhrea; div 1; cir 1; sec 31.

Mar 25; **Herman Fife**; 2m; male; whooping cough; div 22; number 164.

Apr 6; **Sarah Anne Hatcher**; 58y; female; bronchitis; div 2; number 163.

Apr 17; **Infant of Jack Knight**; female; still born; div 2; number 129; two in one grave.

Apr 19; **Infant of Sam Brokis & Wife**; female; still born; div 1; cir 3; sec 64.

Apr 23; **Henry Baker**; 50y; male; neuralgia of heart; div 1; cir 1; sec 22.

Apr 23; **No Name Infant of Lotie Muse**; 6d; female; unknown [cause of death]; div 22; number 165.

Apr 25; **No Name Infant of Mary Chatham**; 1/2d; female; unknown [cause of death]; div 22; number 166.

Apr 28; **Rachel Carter** [NBN: "Entered as Carter"]; 63y; female; asthma; div 2; number 164.

Richmond, Virginia, Mt. Olivet Cemetery Register

[1892 cont.]

May 16; **Harriette Booker** [NBN: "Entered as Booker"]; 50y; female; applexy; div 22; number 167.

May 16; **Bessie May Williams**; 1y 10m; female; cebro spinal menigetis; div 22; number 168.

May 17; **Aggie Mayo**; 62y; female; general debility; div 2; number 165.

May 23; **Sarah Cabell**; 35y; female; natral causes by cororn; div 22; number 169.

Jun 3; **Amelia Ann Johnson**; 48y; female; dropsy of heart; div 1; cir 1; sec 32.

Jun 15; **Louisa Henderson** [NBN: "Entered as Henderson"]; 10m; female; unknown [cause of death]; div 22; number 170.

Jun 22; **Still Born of Henry & Nancy Salley**; female; still birth; div 2; number 165; two in one grave.

Jun 24; **Infant of Carrie Montague**; 14d; female; convulsions; div 22; number 170; two in one grave.

Jun 25; **Wesley Bromskill**; 45y; male; heart disease; div 2; number 166.

Jun 30; **Mary E. Smith**; 9m; female; phthisis; div 22; number 171.

Jul 5; **Louisa Hewlett**; 29y; female; galloping consumption; div 22; number 172.

Jul 10; **Anni Miller** [number written by name "600"]; 43y; female; apoplexsy; div 1; cir 1; sec 22.

[1892 cont.]

Jul 12; **Nellie Harvey**; 54y; female; duber colis; div 22; number 173.

Jul 14; **Infant of M & Susan Henley**; 6m; female; marasmus; div 1; cir 1; sec 22.

Jul 15; **Anni Smith**; 20y; female; acute gastritis; div 2; number 167.

Jul 13; **Infant of Martha Chatham**; div 22; number 174.

Jul 19; **David Andrews**; 27y; male; phthisis; div 2; number 168.

Jul 20; **Floyd Hackney** [NBN: "Entered as Hocking"]; 6m; female [apparent incorrect gender listing]; eyasipilas; div 22; number 175.

Jul 21; **Infant of Addie Pryman**; still birth; div 22; number 176.

Jul 25; **James A. Fields**; 1y 5m 7d; male; apoplexy; div 1; cir 3; sec 54.

Jul 28; **Cora Williams**; 3m; female; dirarrhora; div 22; number 177.

Jul 29; **E. Masse**; male; drowned; div 22; number 178.

Jul 29 **Ruth E. Ross**; 6y; female; malarial fever; div 2; number 169.

Jul 31; **John Johnson**; 18y; male; duis [?]; div 1; cir 3; sec 1.

[Page 16]

Aug 2; **Powhatan Mosby**; 26y; male; pneumonia; div 2; number 170.

Richmond, Virginia, Mt. Olivet Cemetery Register

[1892 cont.]

Aug 3; **Nicholas Mayo**; 70y; male; urania; div 17; sec 2.

Aug 7; **Martha J. Fields**; 35y; female; dropsy; div 2; number 171.

Aug 7; **Osca Tyler**; 1y 6m; male; congestion of brain; div 1; cir 1; sec 33.

Aug 25; **Montessa [?] Perry**; 1y 7m; female; diarahaer; div 22; number 179.

Sep 1; **Ella Wooten**; 2m; marasmus; div 2; number 172.

Sep 4; **Eli Harris**; 1y 8m; male; tuberculosis; div 2; two in one grave.

Sep 6; **Eugen Turner**; 1y 4m; male; marasmus; div 22; number 180.

Sep 11; **Lucy Jane Mosby**; 1y 8m; female; marasmus; div 2; two in one grave.

Sep 11; **Alfred Allen**; 2y 7m; male; malarial fever; div 2; two in one grave.

Sep 16; **Johnnie Hawkins**; 1y 6m; male; marasmus; div 2; number 173.

Sep 19; **Mary Christian**; 18y; female; pleuro pneumonia; div 2; number 174.

Sep 20; **Josephine Gill**; female; meningitis; div 2; number 175.

Sep 20; **Infant** [NBN: "Entered as Unknown"]; div 22; number 181.

[1892 cont.]

Sep 20; **Francis Hall**; 50y; female; heart desiase; div 2; number 177.

Sep 22; **Estell Hill**; 3m; male; diarohara; div 22; number 178; two in one grave.

Sep 29; **Elizabeth Young**; 1y 2m 14d; female; marasmus; div 8; sec 4.

Sep 29; **Ernest Thompson**; 19y; male; consumption; div 22; number 182.

Oct 3; **Hezekiah Hayes**; 3y 3m 21d; male; dysentery; div 2; number 162; two in grave.

Oct 4; **No Name Infant** [NBN: "Under Unknown"]; still born; div 22; number 183.

Oct 11; **Clara Hilton**; 1y 5m; female; dentition; div 2; number 150; two in one grave.

Oct 13; **Herbert R. Jones**; 1y 6m; male; dentition; div 2; number 176.

Oct 17; **Adelaide Griffin**; 52; female; paralysis; div 1; cir 1; sec 25.

Oct 18; **Nannie Harris**; 3y; female; marasmus; div 22; number 184.

Oct 21; **Isham Fields**; 32y; male; chronic diarrhaea; div 1; cir 3; sec 54.

Oct 21; **Octavia Auster** [NBN: "Entered as Auster"]; 4y; female; diphtheretic; div 1; cir 3; sec 54.

Richmond, Virginia, Mt. Olivet Cemetery Register

[1892 cont.]

Nov 7; **Dixin Burnett**; 63; male; endo carditis; div 2; number 178.

Nov 10; **Oti Southall**; 3y; male; accidental burning; div 22; number 185.

Nov 13; **Joseph Finnir** [NBN: "Entered as Fuinor"]; 6y; male; unnon[?] [cause of death]; div 2; number 179.

Nov 16; **Hannibal Henderson**; 50y; male; heart failure; div 2; number 180.

Nov 20; **Sam White**; 43y; male; softening of brain; div 22; number 186.

Dec 1; **Littie Green**; 30y; female; convulsions; div 2; number 181.

Dec 3; **Arthur Burfoot**; 37y; married; pneumonia; Mason.

Dec 7; **Henry Cunningham**; 22y; single; consumption; div 1; cir 1; sec 24.

Dec 11; **Annettia Gregory**; 64y; widow; paralysis; div 2; number 182.

Dec 18; **Delia Robinson**; 48y; consumption; div 2; number 183.

Dec 18; **Jno Holionber** [?]; 67y; dropsy; div 22; number 187.

Dec 25; **Charles H. Johnson**; 1y 3m; male; meningitis; div 2; number 184.

Dec 30; **Joseph Dabney**; 48y; male; pneumonia; div 2; number 185.

1893

Jan 2; **J. M. Branch**; 33y; male; heart disease; div 22; number 188.

Jan 13; **J. H. Coy**; 9y; menegitis; div 2; number 186.

Jan 14; **Mary Simmons**; 55y; widow; heart disease; div 22; number 189.

[Page 17]

Feb 2; **Emily Haden**; 55y; widow; subrt [?] gastritris; div 1; cir 3; sec 66.

Feb 14; **Jack C**; 60y; unknown [cause of death]; div 22; number 190.

Feb 7; **Son of A & Judia Mickens**; 1m 21d; convulsions; div 2; number 188.

Feb 13; **Kate Miller**; 55y; cro" laragetis; div 2; number 189.

Feb 20; **Lee Mason**; 26y; pneumonia; div 2; number 191.

Feb 22; **Jessee Whitteker**; 35y; pneumonia; div 22; number 191.

Feb 25; **James Green**; 35y; married; Bright's disiase; div 22; number 192.

Feb 28; **Estelle Mason**; 1y; marasmus; div 22; number 193.

Mar 1; **Beverly Green**; 63y; consumption; div 22; number 194.

Mar 1; **Bosher Flournoy**; 5y; dropsy; div 2; number 191.

Mar 5; **Thursday Hewlet**; 72y; malariah fever; div 2; number 192.

Richmond, Virginia, Mt. Olivet Cemetery Register

[1893 cont.]

Mar 9; **John Henry Fergerson**; 1y 3m; infantile convulsions; div 22; number 195.

Mar 15; **Sally Cox**; married; rheumatism; div 2; number 193.

Mar 15; **Bing Randolph**; 6m 1d; heart disease; div 22; number 196.

Mar 22; **Still born of Mary Vaughn**; still born [cause of death]; div 22; number 197.

Mar 24; **Volley Burke**; 53y; married; pneumonia; div 2; number 194.

Mar 27; **Edward Harris**; 36y; married; phthisis pulmmalis; div 2; number 195.

Apr 5; **Lee Saunders**; 43y; married; not stated [cause of death]; div 2; number 196.

Apr 13; **Ellen E. Coy**; 9y; pneumonia; div 2; number 197.

Apr 21; **Alice Easters**; 38y; married; chronic; div 2; number 198.

Apr 24; **Marcus Burford**; 39y; married; cebral hemorangue; div 2; number 199.

Apr 25; **A. J. Hankins**; 41y; married; renostored [?] gaul bladder; div 2; number 200.

Apr 27; **Catharine Horks**; 53y; single; typhoid fever; div 2; number 201.

Apr 30; **Nelson Miller;** 53y; widow; dropsy; div 1; cir 1; sec 33.

May 1; **Mary Jane Scott**; 18y; bronchitis; div 2; number 202.

[1893 cont.]

May 3; **Martha Andrews**; 65y; consumption; div 22; number 198.

May 5; **L. L. Price**; 11m; consumption; div 22; number 199.

May 7; **Sarah E. Mason**; 21y; pneumonia; div 2; number 203.

May 8; **Nelson Jackson**; 55y; chronic; div 22; number 200.

May 19; **Chas. Duval Nash**; 2m; consumption; div 22; number 201.

May 19; **Still born of Henrietta Harris**; div 22; number 202.

Jun 10; **Rosa Colman**; 20d; female; div 22; number 203.

Jun 12; **Henrietta Harris**; 40y; female; heart disesiss [?]; div 22; number 204.

Jun 28; **Georgianna Randall**; 4m; diarrhrea; div 22; number 205.

[No date or name]; div 22; number 206.

Jul 2; **No name** [NBN: "Entered as Unknown"]; unknown [cause of death]; div 22; number 207.

Jul 3; **Lena Branch**; 78y; old age; div 22; number 208.

Jul 4; **Antony Jackson**; 52y; diarrhrea; div 22; number 209.

Jul 22; **Mary B. Ross** [NBN: "Entered as Ross"]; 17y; malarial fever; div 22; number 209.

Aug 1; **Rebecca Marshall**; 31y; pelvis peritisiclis [?]; div 1; cir 1; sec 35.

[Page 18]

Richmond, Virginia, Mt. Olivet Cemetery Register

[1893 cont.]

Aug 27; **Charity Hunter**; 25y; puperal fever; div 22; number 214.

Sep 3; **Still born**; [NBN: "Under Unknown"]; 3 hours; premature birth; div 22; number 215.

[Note: the register skips from September 3, 1893 to December 22, 1893.]

Dec 22; **Wm Thomas**; 3m; natural causes; div 22; number 216.

Dec 31; **Peter Monger**; 70y; heart disease; div 22; number 217.

1894

[Note: the register skips from December 31, 1894 to May 27, 1895.]

May 27; **Wm Bruce**; 1y 2m; convulsions; div 22; number 218.

Jun 8; **George Brown**; 10m; infantile diarrhrea; div 22; number 219.

Jun 9; **Bessie Burton** [number after name: "760"]; 4m; diarrhrea; div 22; number 220.

Jun 11; **Billie Montague's fant** [infant]; still born; div 22; number 221.

Jun 14; **Richard Watson**; 54y; hemorrahge; div 22; number 222.

Jul 27; **Mary Gibson**; 16d; inanition; div 22.

Jul 1; **Unknown Infant**; unknown [cause of death]; div 22; number 223.

[1894 cont.]

Jul 20; **Infant of Emma Stuart**; 5m; convulsions; div 22; number 224.

Jul 29; **Infant of Mary Page**; 1m 12d; accidental smothering; div 22; number 225.

Aug 1; **Child of N. L. Ford**; 4y; dysentery; div 22; number 226.

Aug 2; **Amie B. Hicks**; 1y 6m; malaril fever; div 22; number 227.

Aug 5; **Elmira Hilton**; 57y; various heart liver &c.; div 2; number 204.

Aug 11; **Kate Bradshaw**; 40y; convulsions; div 2; number 205.

Aug 11; **Still born of Kate Bradshaw**; still born [cause of death]; div 2; number 205; in grave with its mother. [Kate Bradshaw interred on Aug 11, 1894.]

Aug 18; **Still born of Lizzie Smith**; male; div 22; number 228.

Aug 18; **Henry Lirthey** [?]; [NBN: "Entered as Curttney and Lirthey"]; 3m; male; diarrhrea; div 22; number 229.

Sep 27; **Jeff Powell**; 76y; exhaustion of [illegible]; div 22; number 230.

Sep 27; **Judge House**; 23y; drownding; div 22; number 231.

[No date]; **Davie Coleman**; 10m; cholera infantum; div 22; number 232.

[No date]; **Florence W. Fields**; 10m; convulsions; div 22; number 233.

Oct 7; **Fannie Furgerson**; 76y; abcesses; div 22; number 234.

Richmond, Virginia, Mt. Olivet Cemetery Register

[1894 cont.]

Nov 8; **Eugene Allen**; 3d; bronchitis; div 22; number 235.

Nov 29; **Jennie Johnson**; 22y; pneumonia; div 22; number 237.

Dec 11; **Still born of R. Ceasar & wife**; still born; still born [cause of death]; div 22; number 236.

Dec 17; **Harvey Fowler**; 7m; menegetis; div 22; number 238.

1895

Jan 9; **John H Copeland**; 2m; marasmus; div 22; number 239.

Jan 15; **Alsey Wright**; not given [age]; infernily [?]; div 22; number 240.

[Page 19]

Mar 3; **Nancy Green**; 3m; heart disease; div 22; number 241.

Mar 12; **Mary Kuk**; 19y; tubercolosis; div 22; number 242.

Mar 22; **Jas Gorden**; tubercolosis; div 22; number 243.

Mar 17; **John Dennis**; 9y; not given [cause of death]; div 22; number 244.

Apr 2; **Nancy B. Jones**; 37y; tubercolosis; div 2; number 206.

May 13; **Infant of Mary Gibson**; 0y 0m 0d; still born; div 22; number 245.

May 27; **Fred Murphy** [NBN: "Entered as Murphy"]; 30d; spasms; div 22; number 246.

Jul 4; **Adelia Miller**; 55y; softening of brain; div 22; number 247.

82 Richmond, Virginia, Mt. Olivet Cemetery Register

[1895 cont.]

Jul 22; **Ola Jackson**; 4m; convulsions; div 22; number 248.

Aug 8; **Florence Wingfield**; 1y; convulsions; div 22; number 249.

Sep 4; **Unknown**; 0y 0m 0d; unknown (found dead); div 22; number 250.

Sep 17; **Calvin Keyes** [NBN: "Entered as Keyes"] 6d; inanition; div 22; number 251.

Sep 24; **Jas Washington Cooper**; 6y; whooping cough; div 22; number 252.

Sep 25; **J. Staples**; 2y; typhoid fever; div 22; number 253.

Sep 23; **Ella Johnson**; 38y; hart disease; div 22; number 254.

Sep 30; **Rebecca Milheres**; [NBN: "Entered as Milheres"]; 16d; inanition; div 22; number 255.

[Note: the register skips from September 30, 1895 to Jan --, 1896.]

1896

Jan --; **Mary Freeman**; 3y; capilary bronchitis; div 22; number 256.

Jan 22; **Mary Jones**; 3y; convulsions; div 22.

Feb 15; **Nelson Coleman**; not given [age]; inquest held; div 22; number 257.

Feb 28; **Lilly Ruffin** [NBN: "Entered as Ruffin"]; 18y; tubercolosis; div 22; number 258.

[Note: the register skips from February 28, 1896 to June 13, 1896.]

Richmond, Virginia, Mt. Olivet Cemetery Register 83

[1896 cont.]

Jun 13; **Unknown**; 5m; unknown [cause of death]; div 22; number 259.

Jun 24; **Roberta Anderson**; 2m 19d; diarrhrea; div 22; number 260.

Jun 26; **Josie Lee**; 34y; unknown [cause of death]; div 22; number 261.

Jul 6; **Still born of Mary Richardson**; still birth; div 22; number 262.

Jul 24; **Emma Saunders**; 1y 6m; marasmum; div 22; number 263.

Jul 26; **Still birth of Emily Randolph**; (single); still birth; div 22; number 264.

Jul 27; **Infant of H. Mosely & wife**; not given [age]; convulsions; div 22; number 265.

Jul 30; **Jos Goode**; 43y; dysentery; div 22; number 266.

[Note: the register skips from July 30, 1896 to October 16, 1897 (error 1896 [?])]

Oct 16, 1897 [error – 1896?]; **Still birth from Mary Gibson**; still birth; div 22; number 267.

Oct 23, 1897 [error – 1896?]; **Carrie Staples**; 2y; dysentery; div 22; number 268.

Oct 27; **Allen Cole's infant**; still born; still born [cause of death]; div 22; number 269.

Nov 28; **George Fortune**; 28y; single; phthysis; div 22; number 270.

84   Richmond, Virginia, Mt. Olivet Cemetery Register

[1896 cont.]

Nov 30; **Still born of Mary Page, Lingle**; [NBN: "Entered as Seigle"]; not given [age]; still birth; div 22; number 271.

1897

Jan 1; **Chas Powel**; 38y; married; heart disease; div 22; number 272.

[Page 20]

Jan 3; **Anthony Sharp**; 65y; single; gangrene; div 22; number 273.

Jan 26; **Jas C. Wooldridge**; 61y; married; congestion of lungs; div 22; number 274.

Jan 26; **Catherine Howard**; 64y; widow; inanition; div 22; number 275.

Feb 11; **Hannibal Henderson** [NBN: "Entered as Henderson"]; 7m; male; pneumonia; div 22; number 276.

Mar 11; **Mariah Jones**; 28y; married; pulmonalis; div 22; number 277.

Mar 26; **Tom Orange**; number 278.

Apr 1; **Horace Foster**; 2y 9m; male; menegetis; div 22; number 279.

Apr 24; **Peter Stringfellow**; 61y; married; laryngitis; div 22; number 280.

May 14; **Armstead Thomas**; number 281.

Jun 23 [?]; **Lewis Wells**; number 282.

Richmond, Virginia, Mt. Olivet Cemetery Register

[1897 cont.]

Jun 7; **Charity Ann Moss**; not given [age]; premature birth; div 22; number 283.

Jun 17; **Infant of Lena Edwards** (single); summer diarrhrea; div 22; number 284.

Jun 22; **Infant of Nannie Baker**; 1y 1d; inanition; div 22; number 285.

Jun 14; **Infant of Adelaide Riley** (single); still born; div 22; number 286.

Jun 28; **Still born of Mattie Venable**; male; still born; div 22; number 287.

Jul 8; **Wm Turner**; 51y; married; entero colletis; div 22; number 288.

Jul 14; **Laray Johnson**; 45y; single; syphilisis prypoletis [?]; div 22; number 289.

Jul 14; **Thomas Jackson**; [no additional information provided. Entry very faint – erased?]

Aug 11; **Charlie Nelson**; 6d; male; infantile convulsin; div 22; number 290.

Sep 8; **Adam Brigge**; div 22; number 291.

Oct 24; **Jessee Moosby**; 56y; married; chronic excema [?]; div 2; number 207.

Oct 24; **Rebecca Brinton** [NBN: "Entered as Bunton"]; 70y; married; old age; div 2; number 208.

[1897 cont.]

Nov 18; **Chas Murry**; 28y; single; shot through lung; div 2; number 209.

Nov 9; **Antony Murry**; 35y; single; shot through stomach & bowels; div 2; number 210.

Dec 8; **Squire Bright**; 71y; single; dropsy; div 2 ½ ; number [has "/" mark instead of number].

1898

Feb 16; **Infant of Louis Jackson**; div 22; number 292.

Mar 8; **Sinmord [?] Smith**; 3m; male; natural causes; div 22; number 293.

Mar 11; **[No name]**; div 2; number 211.

Mar 17; **James Gibson**; 5m; male; convulsions; div 22; number 294.

Mar 26; **Belle Williams**; 24y; female; div 1; cir 3, sec 54.

[Page 21]

Apr 1; **Lucious Henley**; 18y; single; spinal menegetis; div 1; cir 1; sec 32.

Apr 23; **Thomas Morton**; 36y; married; phthisis; div 22; number 295.

Apr 23; **Charles Smith**; 2y; male; spinal menegetis; div 22; number 296.

Apr 28; **Preston Harris**; 59y; married; heart disease; div 2; number 212.

[1898 cont.]

May 3; **William Brice**; 60y; married; phthisis pulmonalis; div 22; number 297.

May 4; **William Mathews**; 29y; married; pneumonia; div 2; number 213.

May 14; **Katie Scott**; 16y; single; acute peritonetis; div 2; number 214.

May 19; **Robert Barksdale**; 17y; male; phthisis; div 22; number 298.

Jun 3; **Jno Taylor**; 23y; male; consumption; div 22; number 299.

Jun 5; **Lucinda Walker**; 55y; nervous prostration; div 1; cir 1; sec 36.

Jun 7; **George Coleman**; 5m; male; coroner's case, disease unknown; div 22; number 300.

Jun 13; **Infant of Tom & Mary Morton**; 0y 1m; male; whooping cough; div 22; number 301.

Jun 17; **Floyd Robinson**; 1m; male; dysentery; div 22; number 302.

Jun 18; **W. Richardson** [number after name: "800"]; 4m; male; deficient vitality; div 22; number 303.

Jul 1; **Infant of A. Hankins & Wife**; 15d; male; natural causes; div 2; number 167; in grave with another.

Jul 5; **Wm H. Johnson**; 3y 6m; male; bronchitis; div 1; cir 1; sec 34.

Jul 17; **Annie Finnie**; 26y; div 22; number 304.

[1898 cont.]

Jul 4; **Lewis Bowman**; 98y; married; old age; div 1; cir 1; sec 29.

Jul 5; **Armelia Turpin**; 70y; married; congestion of liver; div 1; cir 1; sec 28.

Jul 15; **Berta Starke**; 1y 1m; female; married; diarrhrea; div 22; number 305.

Jul 19; **Sallie Harris**; 19y; married; phthisis; div 22; number 306.

Jul 27; **C. W. Harris**; 40y; married; entero colitis; div 2; number 215.

Jul 27; **Bennie Meade**; 15y; single; melireal [?] fever; div 2; number 216.

Jul 28; **Wm E. Johnson**; 58y; married; Bright's disease; div 2; number 217.

Jul 28; **Matilda Hankins**; 35y; widow; esteric [?] fever; div 2; number 200; in grave with husband. [A. J. Hankins interred on Apr 25, 1893. Front index lists as A. J. Hawkins.]

Aug 10; **Luellie King**; 6m; female; diarrhrea; div 22; number 307.

Aug 16; **Mary Page**; 31y; single; tubercolosis; div 22; number 308.

Aug 20; **Wm Reed**; 30y; single; effects of being shot; div 22; number 309.

Aug 25; **Premature of T. B. Strayghter**; [NBN: "Entered as Slaughter and Strayghter"]; female; premature birth; div 2; number 203; in grave with another.

[1898 cont.]

Aug 25; **Still born of T. Howlet & wife**; male & female; still born [cause of death]; div 2; number 204; in grave with another.

Aug 28; **Lizzie Smith**; 48y; widow; dropsy; div 2; number 218.

Sep 5; **[No name]**; 50y.

Sep 15; **Mary Booker**; 1y 6m; female; malarial fever; div 2; number 212; in grave with another.

Sep 19; **Lizzie Harris**; 60y; married; dropsy; div 2; number 94; in grave with another.

Sep 22; **Johnson Hire** [NBN: "Entered under H & J"]; 50y; married; paralysis; div 22; number 310; in grave with Eliza Hicks. [Eliza Hicks not listed in register, however a Lizzie Hicks was interred in div 22 on Jan 22, 1878. No grave number was listed.]

Sep 24; **Harrat Nelson**; 55y; widow; fits; div 22; number 311.

[Page 22]

Oct 4; **Still born of Mary J Cook**; not given [age]; female; still born; div 22; number 312.

Oct 14; **Sidney King**; 2y; male; diarrhrea; div 22; number 313.

Oct 14; **M** [no additional name info]; number 218.

Oct 24; **Amanda Morton**; 33y; single; consumption; div 2; number 219.

Oct 30; **Louisa Brooks**; 67y; widow; diarrhrea; div 17; sec 2.

Nov 15; **Rufus Jackson**; 56y; widowed; stone laborer [listed under disease]; div 17; sec 5.

[1898 cont.]

Nov 17; **Rubin Archer**; 60y; widow; heart disease; div 22; number 314; died at alms house.

Nov 18; **Henry Harris**; about 50y; widow; laborer [listed under disease]; div 22; number 115; died at alms house.

Dec 10; **Edward Garland**; 6m; male; malariah; div 1; cir 3; sec 68.

Dec 25; **Delphia Washington**; 40y; widower; cancer; div 2; number 220.

Dec 31; **George Barksdale**; 45y; married; seurus [?] concussine of brain; div 22; number 316; died in alms house.

1899

Jan 11; **Infant of Wm Booker & wife**; 11d; female; natural causes; div 2; grave with another.

Jan 1; **Robert Taylor**; 17y; single; tetamus; div 2; grave 221.

Jan 1; **Richard I Jones**; 14y; single; spiral menagetis; div 1; cir 3; sec 68.

Jan 6; **Elsey Twine**; 54y; widow; rupture of bowels; div 17; sec 5.

Feb 2; **Lottie Belle Allen**; 17y; single; bronchitis; div 1; cir 1; sec 26.

Feb 5; **Still born of Nora Kelly**; still born; male; still born [cause of death]; div 22; number 317.

Feb 6; **L. J. Timberlake**; 42y; widow; phthesis pulmonalis; div 2; number 222.

[1899 cont.]

Feb 12; **F. Lee Foster**; 3m; female; natural cause; div 2; number 223.

Feb 18; **Sophy Nelson**; unknown [age]; widow; shock from cold; div 2; number 224.

Feb 21; **Annie L. Munford**; 25y; single; la guppe; div 2; number 225.

Mar 25; **Erminie Allen**; 5d; female; infantile enclopenia; div 1; cir 1; sec 2.

Apr 23; **Infant of Anna B Trent**; 14d; premature birth; div 22; number 318.

Apr 26; **Amanda Crump**; 49y; general debility; div 2; number 226.

Apr 30; **Georganna Shelton**; 56y; married; pneumonia; div 1; cir 1; sec 40.

May 30; **Still born of Wm Goode & wife**; still born; still born [cause of death]; div 22; number 319.

Jun 6; **Otis Brooks**; 8m; male; acute enteretis; div 22; number 320.

Jun 9; **Jennie Hurt**; 5d; female; acute enteretis; div 1; cir 1; sec 18.

Jun 15; **Jas Parson**; 58y; married; congestion of lungs; div 2; number 227.

Jun 18; **Robert I Mann**; 29y; single; phthisis pulmonalis; div 1; cir 1; sec 30.

[1899 cont.]

Jun 22; **Ada Brooks**; 17y; single; tuberculosis; div 8; sec 4.

Jun 25; **Emma Murry**; 55y; married; anasurca; div 2; buried in grave with son. [Two Murry males were interred in 1897, unable to determine which one is with mother.]

Jun 27; **Delphia Mason**; 49y; married; of uterus; div 8; sec 2.

Jul --; **John H Eaton**; 1y 6m; male; unknown [cause of death]; div 1; cir 1; sec 18.

Jul 12; **Carrie Deane**; 20y; single; phthisis; div 1; cir 1; sec 24.

Jul 26; **Geo W. Fountain**; 20y; single; phthisis; div 1; cir 3; sec 68.

Jul 27; **Aley H. Graham**; 63y; widower; general dibility; div 2; reopened grave on [of ?] wife.

[Page 23]

Aug 8; **J. Sarah Johnson**; 45y; married; heart disease; div 17; sec owned of S. Johnson.

Aug 10; **Willie L. Jenkins**; 7m; male; cause of death not given; div 2; reopened.

Aug 16; **Geo Langston**; 3m; male; congestion of brain; div 1; cir 1; sec 18.

Aug 24; **Betsy Green**; 57y; widow; natural causes; div 2; number 228.

Aug 31; **A. Street**; 7y; female; typhoid fever; div 8; sec 4.

Richmond, Virginia, Mt. Olivet Cemetery Register

[1899 cont.]

Sep 5; **Ida Hickman**; 25y; single; tuberculosis of lungs; div 2; in grave with Sydney Jackson's wife. [Several "Jackson" listings in index. Unable to determine exact individual.]

Sep 13; **Infant of Archer Taylor & wife**; 1m; female; intestinal trouble; div 1; cir 1; sec 33.

Oct 10; **Stepen Brooks**; 45y; single; heart disease; div 22; number 321.

Oct 27; **Mary Howard**; 41y; married; tuberculosis; div 2; number 229.

Nov 4; **Cornelius Finney**; 18y; single; acute tuberculosis; number 322.

Nov 19; **Matilda Marshall**; 23y; single; general infections & tuberculosis; div 1; cir 1; sec 35.

Nov 27; **Richard Howlet**; 42y; single; heart disease; div 22; number 323.

Nov 28; **Agnes R. Jones**; 63y; widow; la grippee; div 8; sec 5.

Dec 5; **Still born of Lelia Robinson**; male; still born; div 22; number 324.

1900

Jan 12; **Kathleen Golden**; 6y 6m 4d; female; convulsions; div 1; cir 1; sec 36.

Jan 15; **Mary Jackson**; 50y; married; pneumonia; div 17; sec 6.

Jan 17; **Elvina Muse**; 2m; female; inanition [?]; div 2; number 145; in grave with another.

[1900 cont.]

Jan 21; **Anna Bell Young**; 27y; married; not given [cause of death]; div 2; number 230.

Jan --; **Granville Robinson**; 98y; widower; old age; div 17; sec 2.

Feb 3; **Jas. Pope**; 49y; married; heart disease; div 2; number 231.

Feb 13; **Davis Jefferson**; 25y; apoplexy; div 2; number 232.

Feb 13; **Still born of David I. Coy & wife**; female; still born; div 22; number 325.

Mar 13; **Nathaniel Christian**; 23y; married; tuberculosis; div 8; sec 2.

Mar 13; **Josephine Johnson**; not given [age]; heart disease; div 22; number 326.

Mar 26; **James Hall**; not given [age]; single; phthisis; div 2; number 233.

Mar 31; **J. M. Brown**; 51y; widower; heart disease; div 1; cir 1; sec 32.

Apr 4; **Jessie Mayr**; 18y; single; pneumonia; div 2; number 234.

Apr 15; **John Moore**; 18y; single; pneumonia; div 22; number 327.

[Page 24]

May 11; **Mary E. Baker**; 10y; female; typhoid fever; div 17; sec 5.
May 14; **Jas Goonele** [NBN: "Entered as Goonele"]; 18y; single; congestive chill; div 22; number 328.

Richmond, Virginia, Mt. Olivet Cemetery Register

[1900 cont.]

May 20; **Rachael Howel**; 8m; female; bronchitis; div 2; number 124; in grave with another.

Jun 6; **Sadie C. Allen**; 1y; convulsions; div 1; cir 3; sec 54.

Jun 15; **Jas. Busby**; 50y; married; dropsy; div 1; cir 3; sec 68.

Jun 17; **Jno Eggleston**; 34y; married; tuberculosis of lungs; div 2; in grave with another.

Jul 18; **Alexander Stratten**; 11m; male; not given [cause of death] not given; div 22; number 329.

Aug 6; **Ruth Williams**; 3y; female; infantile convulsions; div 22; number 330.

Aug 10; **Susan Williams**; 4y; menigetis; div 22; number 331.

Aug 26; **Lelia Johnson**; 27y; tuberolosis; div 17; sec 1.

[Note: the register skips from August 26, 1900 to October 1, 1900.]

Oct 1; **Stillborn of Ema Edmuns** [NBN: "Entered as Edmuns."]; stillborn; male; stillborn [cause of death]; div 22; number 332.

Oct 5; **Jas. Hatcher**; 35y; single; heart disease; div 17; sec 5.

Oct 5; **Amanda Smith**; 55y; widow; apoplexy; div 1; cir 1; sec 21.

Oct 17; **Stillborn Robert Harris & wife**; stillborn; female; still born [cause of death]; div 22; number 333.

96 Richmond, Virginia, Mt. Olivet Cemetery Register

[1900 cont.]

Oct 28; **Rosa Bell Price** [illegible number written after name, appears to be "960"?]; 19y; single; phthisis pulmonales; div 2; number 63.

Nov 21; **Stillborn of David Coy & wife**; stillborn; male; stillborn [cause of death]; div 22; number 334.

Nov 22; **Mary Dozelle**; 3d; female; inanition; div 22; number 335.

Dec 20; **Cary Foster**; 15y; single; bronchitis; div 22; number 336.

Dec 25; **Melissie Powel**; 54y; widow; paralysis; div 2; number 25; two in grave by request.

1901

[Line labeled as heading "Jan 1901" lists grave number 337 only. Div 2 is implied. Apparently the number was entered in error, or name was unknown?]

Jan 10; **Jas Drake**; 35y about; single; pneumonia; div 22; number 338.

Jan 27; **Infant of Jno William & wife**; 6d; female; infantile convulsions; div 22; number 339.

[Note: the register skips from January 27, 1901 to March 22, 1901.]

Mar 22; **Robert Garnett**; 29y; married; pneumonia; div 2; number 235.

Mar 22; **Virginia Coates**; 41y; widow; peritonetis; div 1; cir 3; sec 68.

[1901 cont.]

Apr 26; **Cora B. Powel**; 16y; single; phthisis pulmonales; div 8; sec 2.

May 3; **Charlotte Turner**; 22y; married; puperal fever; div 1; cir 3; sec 66.

May 4; **Julia B. Scott**; 24y; married; tuberculosis; div 22; number 340.

May 10; **Elvira Furgerson**; 48y; widow; carcinoma [?]; div 17; sec 4.

May 13; **Lewis Smith**; 75y; widower; heart disease; div 22; number 341.

May 27; **Still born Bettie Goode**; want of attention; div 22; number 342.

[Page 25]

Jun 3; **Elvira Venable**; 50y; widow; heart disease; div 22; number 343.

Jun 10; **Joseph Brooks**; 64y; widower; pulmonary tuberculosis; div 17; sec 5.

Jun 11; **Elvira Irvin**; 4m; female; accidental drownding; div 22; reopened grave.

Jun 19; **Parthenia Cunningham**; 48y; married; hemorrhage uterus; div 1; cir 1; sec 24.

Jun 20; **Mary Mason**; 28y; single; tuberculosis; div 17; sec 10.

Jun 22; **Joseph Price**; 35y; married; pulmonary hemorage; div 22; number 344.

[1901 cont.]

Jun 26; **Thos Walke**; 23y; single; unknown [cause of death]; div 2; reopened.

Jun 29; **Nellie Prosser**; 51y; married; apoplexy; div 2; number 236.

Jun 29; **Anthony Binga Sr**; 86y; married; gen. debility; div 1; cir 1; sec 20.

Jun 30; **Infant of Major Furgerson**; 2m; female; want of vitality; div 22; number 345.

Jun 30; **Mary D. Turner**; 2m; female; diarrhoea; div 1; cir 1; sec 21.

Jul 11; **George Gray**; not given [age]; single; heart disease; div 8; sec 2.

Jul 16; **Infant of Jno Eaton & wife**; 5d; male; ininction; div 1; cir 1; sec 18.

Jul 13; **Isam Woody**; 18y; single; pneumonia; div 11; number 32.

Jul 27; **Johnson Gary**; 68y; married; dropsy; div 17; sec 10.

Jul 30; **Betsy Ann Washington**; 90y; widow; pneumonia; div 1; cir 1; sec 32.

~~Aug 5; **Peter Patterson**; 78y; widow; paralysis & operation; div 22.~~ Turned over to the atorny[?] Board of Va.

Aug 12; **Lucy L. Moon**; 56y; married; crucinonia; div 1; cir 3; sec 64.

Aug 14; **Fannie Johnson**; 53y; married; carcinonia of pancreas; div 1; cir 3; sec 1.

Richmond, Virginia, Mt. Olivet Cemetery Register

[1901 cont.]

Aug 16; **Mary Crear**; 70y; widow; dropsy; div 2; number 237.

Aug 27; **Robert Jones**; 35y; married; accident; div 17; sec 6.

Aug 29; **Sissie Powel**; 40y; married; chronic; div 1; cir 1; sec 18.

Sep 3; **Jane Ross** [NBN: "Entered as Ross"]; 45y; married; appoplexy; div 2; number 238.

Sep 9; **Alma Holmes**; 23y; married; tubercolosis; div 8; sec 1.

Sep 16; **Bansey Winston**; 4y; female; marasmus; div 1; cir 3; sec 68.

Oct 16; **Mike Barnes**; 37y; married; drownding; div 8; sec 1.

Oct 18; **Aubrey Wiley**; 1y; male; infantile convulsions; div 2; grave with another.

Oct 28; **Sarah Meyo**; 48y; married; apoplexy; div 17; sec 2.

Oct 31; **Joshua Wrenn**; 36y; married; gastric calarrh [?]; div 2; number 239.

Oct 31; **Georgianna Randolph**; 85y; widow; paralysis; div 8; sec 2.

Nov 10; **Jessee Thomas**; 56 or 58y; married; paralysis; div 1; cir 3; sec 68.

Nov 13; **Marie Murry**; 5y; female; burns; div 2; with another.

Nov 26; **Sam'l Brooks**; 56y; married; paralysis; div 1; cir 3; sec 66.

[1901 cont.]

Nov 29; **John H. Tubbs**; 46y; married; phthisis; div 1; cir 3; sec 58.

[Page 26]

Dec 3; **Wyatt Dodson**; 28y; single; abscess on liver; div 2; on top of another.

Dec 10; **Algie Copeland**; 23y; single; phthisis; div 1; cir 3; sec 54.

Dec 12; **Monero Miller**; 36y; married; paralysis; div 17; sec 6.

Dec 13; **Cornelius Woolridge**; 43y; married; congestion; div 8; sec 4.

Dec 15; **Granville Robinson**; 50y; single; cerohisis of liver; div 17; sec 2.

Dec 22; **Marian Colis**; 3y; female; pneumonia; div 8; sec 3.

Dec 23; **Stephen Keye**; 1m; inanition; div 22; number 346; pauper.

Dec 29; **Inf. of Richard Branch**; 1y 6m; female; congestion; div 22; number 347.

1902

Jan 13; **Granville Olphin**; 47y; married; heart disease; div 17; sec 10.

Jan 16; **Alexander Johnson**; 50y; married; heart disease; div 17; sec 4.

Jan 23; **Elizabeth Bright**; 36y; married; henoragues [?]; div 2; in grave on [illegible].

Richmond, Virginia, Mt. Olivet Cemetery Register

[1902 cont.]

Jan 28; **Still born of H & M Threet** [NBN: "Entered as Threet"]; still born; div 2; in a reopened grave.

Jan 29; **Gracie Murray**; 15y; single; consumption; div 1; cir 1; sec 21.

[Costs started being listed in register.]

Feb 9; **Blanche Hill**; 17y; single; tuberculosis; div 2; number 45; with Lizzie Harris; cost 4. [Lizzie Harris was interred on Sep 19, 1898.]

Feb 10; **Eddie Smith**; 1y 2m 2d; peritonitis; div 17; section 4; cost 2.

Feb 13; **Mary E. Freeman**; 26y; married; hemoragues [?]; div 17; section 6; cost 4.

Feb 13; **Infant of Wm H. Freeman**; in intero; in coffin & grave with mother.

Feb 15; **Lucy Christian**; 56y; widow; burns; div 1; cir 1; section 35; cost 4.

Feb 17; **Lucy Brooks**; 70y; widow; heart disease; div 1; cir 3; section 66; cost 4.

Feb 18; **Ellen Hays**; 60y; widow; heart disease; div 8; section 1; cost 4.

Feb 20; **Eliza Bailey**; 59y; widow; mental insuffiency; div 1; cir 3; sec 54; cost 4.

Feb 25; **Louisa Johnson**; 42y; pneumonia; div 1; cir 1; sec 21; cost 4.

[1902 cont.]

Feb 27; **Saml & Laura Booker [infant of]**; 2m; male; capilary bronchitis; div 2; number 72; reopened grave; cost 2.

Mar 1; **George Dabney**; 44y; married; accidentally killed; div 17; sec 1; cost 4 00.

Mar 4; **W. H. Giles**; 65y; widower; cardiac dropsey; colored Mason's section; cost 4.

Mar 4; **Algie Davis Coleman**; 17y; single; cebral congestion; div 2; number 17; with another; cost 4.

Mar 8; **Wm A. Lewis**; 7m 21d; male; congestion; div 2; with another; cost 2.

Mar 10; **Rosa Ross** [NBN: "Entered as Rosa Ross"]; 21y; widow; tuburcolosis; div 1; cir 1; sec 22; cost 4.

Mar 25; **Percel Miller**; 2y 1m 3d; single; pneumonia; div 17; sec 6; cost 2.

Mar 29; **Elizabeth Brown**; 52y; unknown [cause of death]; div 1; cir 3; sec 54; cost 4.

Apr 3; **Wm Lewis**; 27y; married; chronic; div 1; cir 3; sec 68; cost 4.

Apr 7; **Jacob Jones**; 49y; married; pneumonia; div 8; sec 5; cost 4.

Apr 8; **Melvina E. Andrews**; 10y; single; double pneumonia; div 2; reopened grave; cost 2.

Apr 19; **Sidney Allen**; 55y; married; pneumonia; div 17; sec 4; cost 4.

Richmond, Virginia, Mt. Olivet Cemetery Register 103

[1902 cont.]

May 1; **Jno P. West**; 1y 5m; male; broncho pneumonia; div 1; cir 1; sec 23; cost 2.

May 22; **Lee Gordon**; 26y; married; heart failure; div 2; number 259; cost 4.

May 26; **M. Eva Rhone** [NBN: "Entered at Rhone"]; 6m; female; pneumonia; div 22; number 348; cost 0 00.

[Page 27]

Jun 12; **John Miles**; 60y about; widower; appolexy; div 17; sec 4; cost 4.

Jun 15; **Unknown**; unknown [age]; unknown [cause of death]; div 22; number 349; cost 0 00.

Jun 16; **Edwd Johnson**; 76y; male; cholera infantum; div 3; number 1; cost 4.

Jun 20; **Carrie L. Fitz**; 7m 29dy; female; cholera infantum; div 1; cir 1; sec 29; cost 2.

Jun 23; **Lillie Johnson**; 1m 8d; female; cholera infantum; div 1; cir 1; sec 35; cost 2.

Jun 26; **Lucy Ann Johnson**; 1m 10d; female; maramus; div 1; cir 3; sec 1; cost 2.

Jul 3; **Conrad Bacon**; 6m 2d; male; cholera infantum; div 2; number 209; reopened; cost 2.

Jul 7; **Infant of Mary L. Carrington**; 4d; female; icterius [?]; div 22; number 350; cost 0 00.

104 Richmond, Virginia, Mt. Olivet Cemetery Register

[1902 cont.]

Jul 7; **Infant of Robert Harris & Wife**; 5d; female; premature birth [cause of death]; div 2; number 137; with another; cost 2.

Jul 13; **Cora Edmons**; 5m; female; cholera infantum; div 2; number 68; reopened grave; cost 2.

Jul 17; **Infant of Bettie Goode**; premature; male; premature [cause of death]; div 22; number 351; cost 0 00.

Jul 19; **Willie Robert Jones**; 1y 8m; male; typhoid fever; div 2; number 17; with another; cost 2 00.

Jul 23; **Rosabella Robinson**; 2y 8m; female; infantum; div 22; number 352; cost 0 00.

Aug 3; **Mary E. Mire** [NBN: "Entered as Mire"]; 6m; female; pertussis; div 1; cir 1; number 18; cost 2 00.

Aug 3; **Eugene Powel** [number after name: "1600"]; 26y; single; double pneumonia; div 1; cir 1; number 28; cost 4 00.

Aug 18; **Ira Waddelle**; 15y; single; typhoid fever; div 1; cir 1; number 30; cost 4 00.

Aug 21; **Estelle Staples**; 2y; female; infantile convulsions; div 2; number 133; with another; cost 2 00.

Aug 22; **Peter Miller**; 39y; married; heart disease; div 1; cir 1; number 32; cost 4 00.

Aug 28; **Julia Ann Baugh**; 60y; married; gen debility; div 1; cir 3; sec 54; cost 4 00.

Aug 28; **Garnett Wm Fleming**; 27y; married; tuberculosis pulmonary; div 1; cir 3; sec 64; cost 4 00.

Richmond, Virginia, Mt. Olivet Cemetery Register

[1902 cont.]

Sep 1; **Eddie Thompson**; 33y; single; emphysema; div 1; cir 1; sec 40; cost 4.

Sep 1; **Alexander Benj. Hopes**; 3m; male; marasmus; div 8; sec 4; cost 2.

Sep 6; **Crenshaw Jackson**; 10m; male; teething; div 8; sec 2; cost 2.

Sep 9; **Wm Carington**; 3y; male; entero colitis; div 22; number 353; cost 0 00.

Sep 10; **Eliza Cunningham inf** [NBN: "Entered as Infant of"]; 1d; female; inanition; div 2; number 37; with another; cost 2.

Sep 11; **Mary Jane Coles**; 40y; widow; unknown [cause of death]; div 1; cir 1; sec 21; cost 4.

Sep 11; **Mary A. Hill**; 16y 5m 15d; single; meningitis; div 3; number 2; cost 4.

Sep 11; **Green Lipscomb**; 54y; married; absess of liver; div 1; cir 1; sec 18; cost 4.

Sep 14; **Sarah Jones**; 58y; widow; gastro enteritis; div 2; number 11; with another; cost 4.

Sep 16; **Wm Christian**; 2y 6m; male; cholera infantum; div 1; cir 1; sec 35; cost 2.

Sep 17; **Cl Jones**; 26y; married; explosion; div 17; sec 2; cost 4.

Sep 17; **Fannie Bock** [NBN: "Entered as Bock and Rock"]; 49y; married; congestion of lungs; div 3; number 3, cost 4.

[1902 cont.]

Oct 13; **Augustus Brown**; 60y; widower; diarrhoea; div 17; sec 10; cost 4.

Oct 14; **Geo Hargrove**; 36y; married; bursting of blood vessle; div 2; number 7; reopened; cost 4.

Oct 18; **Curtis Fergusson**; 1m 15d; male; pneumonia; div 2; number 32; with another; cost 2.

[Page 28]

Nov 27; **Robert Armstead**; 60y; married; congestion of liver; div 2; number 13; reopened; cost 4.

Nov 29; **Thos. H. Mann**; 60y; married; hepatitis; div 17; sec 6; cost 4.

Dec 14; **Lucile A. Wilder**; 9m; female; bronchal pneumonia; div 17; sec 10; cost 2.

Dec 16; **Joseph Johnson**; 50y; male; nephintis; div 1; cir 1; sec 25; cost 4.

Dec 18; **Smith Richmond** [NBN: "Entered under both R & S"]; 1y 2m 28y; male; bronchal pneumonia; div 1; cir 1; sec 18; cost 2.

Dec 24; **Jas Haden**; 32y; single; convulsions; div 1; cir 3; sec 66; cost 4.

Dec 28; **Elizabeth Blackwell**; 65y; asthema; div 17; sec 1; cost 4.

Dec 31; **Horace Jackson**; 38y; phthesis; div 2; number 85; with another; cost 4.

1903

Jan 3; **Margaret Allen**; 35y; married; mania; div 1; cir 1; sec 33; cost 4.

Jan --; **Howard Lee Washington**; 1m 12d; male; unknown [cause of death]; div 2; number 98; with another; cost 2.

Jan 11; **Edmond Turpin**; 70y; male; senility; div 1; cir 1; sec 28; cost 4.

Jan 15; **Gladys Hatcher**; 8y; single; dropsy & kidney trouble; div 2; number 85; with another; cost 2.

Feb 1; **Willis Austin**; 5m; male; hydrocephalis; div 2; number 83; with another; cost 2.

Feb 14; **Annie B. Coleman**; 2y; female; pneumonia; div 2; number 27; with another; cost 2.

Feb 19; **Rosa Davis**; 26y; single; tuberculosis; div 3; number 4; cost 4.

Feb 26; **Catharine Fitzgerald**; 2y; female; bronchitis; div 2; number 79; with another; cost 2.

Mar 4; **Ruth Patterson**; 7y; female; natur [?] weekness; div 2; number 183; with another; cost 2.

Mar 5; **Chas Harris**; 1y; male; pneumonia; div 2; number 131; with another; cost 2.

Mar 13; **Lelia Kinder**; 26y; married; tuberculosis; div 2; number 38; with another; cost 4.

Mar 16; **China Harvey**; 70y; widower; asthma; div 2; number 47; with another; cost 4.

108 Richmond, Virginia, Mt. Olivet Cemetery Register

[1903 cont.]

Mar 23; **Sally Boyd**; not given [age]; widow; asthma; div 17; sec 4; cost 4.

Mar 24; **Jas. Foster**; 18y; single; accidental drownding; div 3; number 5; cost 4.

Apr 1; **Newborn of Rosa Johnson**; inanition; div 22; number 354; pauper.

Apr 4; **Nancy Logan**; 50y; widow; asthma; div 3; number 6; cost 4.

Apr 16; **Geo Tinsley & wife** [NBN: "Entered as Infant of"]; 9d; female; unknown [cause of death]; div 1; cir 1; sec 18; cost 2.

Apr 20; **Jas Green & wife** [NBN: "Entered as Infant of"]; 21d; male; premature; div 2; number 108; with another; cost 2.

Apr 27; **Wm Jackson**; 46y; single; peritonitis; div 1; cir 3; sec 68; cost 4.

Apr 27; **Sanl' Hastings**; 53y; married; natural, insufficiency; div 2; number 33; with another; cost 4.

May 6; **Kate McKenzie**; 15y 1m 29d; single; phthisis pulmonalis; div 2; number 17; cost 4.

May 1; **Alice Brown**; 50y; widow; endocarditis; div 1; cir 1; sec 21; cost 4.

May 1; **Emmit Flemming**; 1y 1m; male; heart failure; div 2; sec number 13; with another; cost 2.

May 5; **Francis Jackson**; 55y; female; heuriphigia [?]; div 3; number 7; cost 4.

Richmond, Virginia, Mt. Olivet Cemetery Register

[1903 cont.]

[Page 29]

May 11; **Thos Monroe**; 50y; married; unknown [cause of death]; div 2; number 48; with another; cost 4.

May 11; **Saml Patterson**; 52y; married; osteo sarcoma; div 2; number 76; with another; cost 4.

May 11; **Paulina Taylor**; 70y; widow; pneumonia; div 1; cir 1; sec 68; cost 4.

May 22; **Elizabeth Cunningham**; 56y; married; tuberculosis; div 1; cir 1; sec 18; cost 4.

May 24; **Herman Hilton**; 2d; male; unknown [cause of death]; div 2; number 66; with another; cost 2.

May 30; **Chas. Mosby**; 38y; single; menengitis; div 2; number 32; with another; cost 4.

Jul 6; **Wilhart Washington**; 18/12y; single; gastro enteritis; div 2; number 105; with another; cost 4.

Jul 8; **Louise James**; 9m; female; cholera infantum; div 1; cir 3; sec 66; number 105; with another; cost 2.

Jul 8; **Mrs. Martha Height**; 23y; married; pulmonary tumor; div 1; cir 1; sec 32; cost 4.

Jul 9; **Still born of Jas & M. Height**; stillborn; buried in coffin with mother; cost 0. [Mrs. Martha Height interred on Jul 8, 1903.]

Jul 11; **Nellie Harris**; 15y; single; pneumonia; div 22; number 355; pauper.

[1903 cont.]

Jul 20; **Premature of Mary Hence** [NBN: "Entered as Hence"]; premature; div 22; number 356; pauper.

Jul 24; **Alex Green**; 2m; male; enteritis; div 1; cir 1; sec 35, cost 2.

Jul 26; **Infant of Nettie Goode**; still birth; still birth [cause of death]; div 22; number 357; p[auper].

Jul 27; **John E. Hill**; 2y 3m 8d; male; cancreum [?] oris [?]; div 2; number 54; with another; cost 2.

Jul 27; **Gertrude Moore**; 9m; female; entiro colitis; div 2; number 116; with another; cost 2.

Jul 29; **Joe Blakley**; not given [age]; unknown [marital status]; typhoid; div 22; number 358; pauper.

Aug 1; **Spencer T. Hall**; 60y; widower; dysentery; div 2; number 83; with another; cost 4.

Aug 9; **Infant of Mary Edmons**; 0y 0m 0d; female; still birth; div 22; number 359; pauper.

Aug 22; **Lottie May Armstead**; 16y 3m; female; pocrtes [?]; div 1; cir 1; sec 24; cost 4.

Aug 24; **Bessie Bowen**; 56y; female; enteretis; div 2; number 102; with another; cost 2.

Aug 29; **Millie Bullock**; 14y 1m 16d; single; tubercolosis; div 1; cir 1; sec 29; cost 4.

Sep 22; **Jas. R. Johnson**; 48y; married; typhoid fever; div 2; number 14; with another; cost 4.

[1903 cont.]

Sep 25; **Mary Royall Johnson**; 2y; female; unknown [cause of death]; div 22; number 360; order of meyeor; pauper.

Sep 28; **Eliza Jane Jackson**; 26y; phahpitis [?]; div 17; sec 3; cost 4.

Oct 5; **Mathews Allen**; 5y; male; convulsions; div 2; number 88; with another; cost 2.

Oct 7; **Jennie Royall**; 16y 6m; single; phthesis pulmonalis; div 2; number 104; with another; cost 4.

Oct 14; **Adelia West**; 6m; female; natural [cause of death]; div 22; number 361; ordered by meyor; pauper.

Oct 21; **Dan'l Pincham**; not given [age]; widower; R. R. accident; div 1; cir 3; sec 64; cost 4.

Oct 25; **Leslie Irvine**; 20m; capillary bronchitis; div 22; number 362; pauper.

Oct 26; **Jennie Jones**; 50y; married; meningitis; div 17; sec 2; pauper; cost 4.

Nov 5; **Henry Sulley**; not given [age]; married; phthisis; div 2; number 83; with another; cost 4.

Nov 9; **Blanche Booker**; 16y; single; pneumonia; div 2; number 62; with another; cost 4.

Nov 10; **Jas. A. Baugh**; 17y; single; acute tubercolosis; div 1; cir 3; sec 66; cost 4.

Nov 13; **Maria Bollings** [NBN: "Entered as both B & R"]; 60y; widow; apoplexy; div 17; sec 1; cost 4.

[1903 cont.]

Nov 16; **Infant of T. & A. Goode**; not given [age]; inanition; div 2; number 8; reopened; with another; cost 2.

[Page 30]

Nov 19; **Chas H. Walthall**; 29y; single; typhoid fever; div 1; cir 3; sec 64; cost 4.

Nov 20; **Richard Fowlkes**; 47y; married; nephritis; div 2; sec 11; with another; cost 4.

Dec 1; **Sallie Crampton**; 16y; single; syphilis; div 1; cir 1; sec 22; with another; cost 4.

Dec 3; **Alma Lee Brooks**; 1y 9m 12d; pneumonia; div 2; number 62; with another; cost 2.

Dec 4; **John Roane**; 24y; married; tubercolisis; div 2; number 86; with father; cost 4.

Dec 19; **Henry Brown**; 42y; widower; from fall [cause of death]; div 8; sec 1; cost 4.

Dec 21; **Still born of Eliza Jackson;** [NBN: "not married"]; premature birth; div 22; number 363; order of mayor; pauper.

1904

Jan 1; **Florence Graham**; 24y; single; phthisis pulmonalis; div 2; number 88; with another; cost 4.

Jan 1; **Elizabeth Robinson**; 6m; single; broncho pneumonia; div 3; number 2; with another; cost 2.

Jan 2; **Infant of Henry & Mary Threat**; still born; male; still born [cause of death]; div 1; cir 1; number 18; cost 2.

Richmond, Virginia, Mt. Olivet Cemetery Register

[1904 cont.]

Jan 4; **Tomy Jones** [number after name: "1100"]; 27y; single; facture of spine; div 3; number 8; cost 4.

Jan 8; **Mary Coleman**; 4m; female; pneumonia; div 2; number 108; with another; cost 2.

Jan 17; **No name (Smith W. E. L.)** [NBN: "Entered as an infant of W. E. L. Smith's]; none [age]; male; premature; div 1; cir 1; sec 29; cost 2.

Jan 19; **Jas H. Haxell;** 75y; widower; brain trouble; div 2; number 10; with another; cost 4.

Jan 19; **Mrs. Anna Jefferson**; 32y; married; tuberculosis; div 2; number 14; with another; cost 4.

Jan 20; **Jas Dunn;** 20y; single; tuberculosis; div 22; number 364; pauper.

Jan 26; **John Bundy**; 60y; married; nephritis; div 17; sec 1; cost 4.

Jan 29; **Florence G. Smith**; 30y; married; nufections [?] nausea; div 17; sec 6; cost 4.

Jan 31; **Arthur Taylor**; 27d; male; intsl. obstruction; div 2; sec 14; number 80; with another; cost 2.

Feb 1; **A. J. Anderson**; 54y; married; heart disease; div 2; number 33; with another; cost 4.

Feb 20; **Charlotte White**; 40y; single; apopley; div 2; number 69; with another; cost 4.

Feb 23; **Frank Smith**; 35y; married; burns; div 1; cir 1; sec 18; cost 4.

[1904 cont.]

Mar 8; **Lousa Johnson**; 59y; widow; cataach [?] of stomach; div 2; number 38; with another; cost 4.

Mar 18; **Bruce Dancey**; 2m; male; menengitis; div 22; number 365; order of mayor; pauper.

Apr 1; **Lelia Robinson**; 28y; single; pneumonia; div 2; number 86; with another; cost 4.

Apr 4; **Virginia Rose**; 47y; married; nephthretis; div 8; sec 1; cost 4.

Apr 12; **Olivia Miller**; 2y; female; div 2; number 9; with another; cost 2.

Apr 15; **Lewis Johnson**; 61y; married; convulsions; div 17; sec 3; cost 4.

Apr 21; **Oscar Hobson**; 4m; male; pneumonia; div 2; number 14; with another; cost 2.

Apr 28; **J. Louise Logan**; 1y 12d; female; hydrocephalus; div 1; cir 1; sec 29; cost 2.

[Note: Register did not contain pages 31 and 32. Apparently entries continued on page 33 without a gap in interment dates.]

[Page 33]

May 1; **Infant of J & L Coleman**; still born; female; still born [cause of death]; div 1; sec 18; cost 2.

May 3; **Ruth Randolph**; 2y 4m; female; bronchitis; div 2; number 71; cost 2.

Richmond, Virginia, Mt. Olivet Cemetery Register

[1904 cont.]

May 6; **Henry Edloe** [NBN: "Entered as Edloe"]; 60y; married; hermia sh [?]; div 2; sec 9; with another; cost 4.

May 9; **Earnest Hughes**; 21y; single; fracture of skull; div 1; cir 1; sec 35; cost 4.

May 10; **Robert Pascall**; 39y; married; pneumonia; div 1; cir 1; sec 40; cost 4.

May 21; **Henrietta Edmons**; 56y; married; apoplexy; div 2; number 108; with another; cost 4.

May 28; **Maria Deane**; 52y; widow; pulmonary hemorage; div 2; number 72; cost 4.

Jun 4; **Henry Jeeter**; 25y; single; tubuculosis; div 17; sec 4; cost 4.

Jun 13; **Herbert Green**; 4m; male; intero colitis; div 2; number 18; cost 2.

Jun 16; **Eliza Goode**; 32y 11m 12d; married; malarial fever; div 8; sec 4; cost 4.

Jun 18; **Emma Willson**; 29y; not known [single or married]; heart disease; div 1; sec 25; cost 4.

Jul 2; **Edward Bradley**; 3y 13d; male; cholera infantum; div 1; cir 1; sec 22; cost 2.

Jul 4; **Infant of Mary Logan**; 2y 13d; female; entiro colotis; div 3; number 6; with another; cost 2.

Jul 10; **Clarence Dance**; 6m; single; cholera infantum; div 2; number 123; cost 2.

[1904 cont.]

Jul 15; **Effie Christmas**; 1y 6m; female; enteretis; div 2; number 209; with another; cost 2.

Jul 17; **Margarette Bacon**; 6m; female; marasmus; div 2; number 215; cost 2.

Jul 17; **Jas T. Fitz**; 1y 29d; male; entiro colitis; div 2; number 4; with another; cost 2.

Jul 18; **Maria Howlet**; 10y 14d; female; pneumonia; div 1; cir 1; sec 40; cost 2.

Jul 22; **Lelia Isabelle Gordon**; 2y 6m 1d; female; cholera infantum; div 2; number 252; cost 2.

Jul 22; **Abner Baker**; 69y; married; dysentery; div 2; number 202; cost 4.

Jul 26; **Clara Williams**; 56y; widow; apoplexy; div 2; number 52; with another; cost 4.

Jul 27; **Sandrum Henderson**; 56y; married; apoplexy; div 1; cir 1; sec 21; cost 4.

Jul 27; **Vernon L. Edmonson**; 4y 12d; male; cholera infantum; div 2; number 73; cost 2.

Aug 3; **Police Hamlin**; 82y; widower; apoplexy; div 17; sec 3; cost 4.

Aug 4; **David Goode**; 32y; married; chronic; div 8; sec 2; cost 4.

Aug 8; **Florence Smith**; 15m 18d; female; entero colitis; div 2; number 36; with another; cost 2.

Richmond, Virginia, Mt. Olivet Cemetery Register

[1904 cont.]

Aug 12; **Peter M. Briggs**; 25y 25d; single; consumption; div 2; number 73; with another; cost 4.

Aug 19; **Florence E. Hilton**; 17y 2m; single; consumption; div 2; number 48; with another; cost 4.

Aug 21; **Adam Harris**; 60y; married; mitral stenosis; div 1; cir 1; sec 35; cost 4.

Aug 22; **John Grimm**; 51y; married; pelvic jentilie [?]; div 1; cir 1; sec 29; cost 4.

Aug 23; **Susie B. Fountain**; 26y; single; dysentery; div 3; number 6; with another; cost 4.

Sep 3; **Sallie Wiley**; 68y; widow; enteretis; div 1; cir 1; sec 28; cost 4.

Sep 7; **Annie Finney**; 18y; single; enteretis; div 2; sec 87; with another; cost 4.

Sep 8; **Wm Richardson**; 9m; male; improper food; div 2; sec 16; with another; cost 2.

Sep 14; **Peter Howlet**; 71y; married; asthma; div 17; sec 3 [?]; cost 4.

Sep 16; **Twins of Henry M[?]free & Billie Gray**; still born; div 22; number 366; order of mayor; cost 0. [Front index lists as "Gray, Henry, Winfree & Bettie Gray, infant of."]

Sep 17; **John Brown**; 38y; married; asthma; div 8; sec 2; cost 4.

[1904 cont.]

[Page 34]

Sep 28; **Lizzie Sneed**; 39y 5m 9d; single; consumption; div 2; number 39; with another; cost 4.

Sep 27; **Biunthel Munford**; 3y; single; not given [cause of death]; div 2; number 52; with another; cost 2.

Sep 29; **Sarah E. Hillard**; 3m 19d; female; bronchitis; div 2; number 2; with another; cost 2.

Oct 4; **Howard L. Randolph**; 1y 3m 21d; male; entero colotis; div 2; number 77; with another; cost 2.

Oct 8; **Dorothea Jones**; 1y 4m 25d; female; bronchitis; div 2; number 38; with another; cost 2.

Oct 10; **Geo Allen Price**; 38y 9m 13d; single; tubercolisis; div 17; sec 2; cost 4.

Oct 19; **Bessie Pride**; 2m; female; asthma; div 2; number 35; with another; cost 2.

Oct 29; **Elizabeth Young**; 6m 6d; female; whooping cough; div 2; number 105; with another; cost 2.

Nov 1; **Walker Johnson**; 37y; married; typhoid fever; div 3; number 9; cost 4.

Nov 2; **Margaret Worsham**; 45y; married; hemorauge of lungs; div 17; sec 4; cost 4.

Nov 4; **Blanche Britton**; 16y; single; tubercolosis; div 3; number 70; cost 4.

[1904 cont.]

Nov 7; **Wm Branch**; 58y; married; gastritis; div 2; number 107; with another; cost 4.

Nov 12; **Fred Branch**; 33y; single; paralysis; div 22; number 366; pauper; order of meyur.

Nov 13; **Walter Taylor**; 21y; not given [marital status]; not given [cause of death]; div 1; cir 1; sec 28; cost 4.

Nov 15; **Eliza Terry**; 55y; married; heart disease; div 2; sec number 68; with another; cost 4.

Nov 17; **Arthur H. Mosby**; 1y 2m; male; bronchitis; div 2; number 59; cost 2.

Nov 18; **Iseah Locket**; 17y; single; pneumonia; div 1; cir 1; sec 21; cost 4.

Dec 1; **Arabella Powel**; 26y; single; endocaditis; div 1; cir 1; sec 30; cost 4.

Dec 2; **Cyphus Roberts**; 30y; single; nephritis; div 2; number 211; with another; cost 4.

Dec 3; **Eliza Moseley**; 85y; widow; apoplexy; div 3; number 11; cost 4.

Dec 17; **Robt Branch** [NBN: "Entered as infant of Father's name"]; 1y 7m; male; congestion of brain; div 1; cir 1; sec 22; cost 2.

Dec 18; **Amanda Hillard**; not given [age]; married; acute nephritis; div 1; cir 1; sec 25; cost 4.

Dec 22; **Robert W. Harris**; 54y; married; black smith; div 1; cir 1; sec 19; cost 4.

Richmond, Virginia, Mt. Olivet Cemetery Register

[1904 cont.]

Dec 27; **Geo. Henry Taylor**; 20y; single; unknown, natural [cause of death]; div 2; number 28; with another; cost 4.

Dec 29; **Chas Robinson**; 1y 6m; male; entero colitis; div 2; number 202; with another; cost 2.

Dec 29; **Jas Pennock**; 21y; single; acute nepthitis; div 1; cir 1; sec 33; cost 4.

1905

Jan 1; **Mary Hackney**; 53y; married; [—?] insufficiency; div 1; cir 1; sec 27; cost 4.

Jan 3; **Norman Stultz**; 8y; male; septo meningitis; div 2; number 113; with another; cost 2.

Jan 13; **Norville Richardson**; 33y; married; asthma; div 2; number 208; with another; cost 4.

Jan 20; **Ophelia Shaw**; 1y; female; pneumonia; div 3; number 8; with another; cost 2.

Jan 20; **Immanuel Gibson**; 65y; widower; ac. gastro enteritis; div 1; cir 1; sec 29; cost 4.

Jan 24; **Sidney E. Giles**; 30y; valvulus [?]; div 17; sec 3; cost 4.

Jan 29; **Cora Lee Gipson**; 1y; female; convulsions; div 2; number 191; with another; cost 2.

Jan 29; **Wise Burks**; 50y; married; typhoid fever; div 8; sec 1; cost 4.

[1905 cont.]

[Page 35]

Feb 1; **Roswell Branch**; 3y; male; lung trouble; div 3; number 7; with another; cost 2.

Feb 8; **John Whitehead**; 2y; male; pithesis; div 1; sec 18; cost 2.

Feb 9; **Pearl Davis**; 26y; single; tubercolosis; div 2; number 216; with another; cost 4.

Feb 13; **John Davis**; 50y; married; pneumonia; div 1; sec 66; cost cost 4.

Feb 19; **Mary J. Holmes**; 25y; married; pneumonia; div 1; sec 23; cost 4.

Feb 20; **Lewis A. Hall**; 1m; male; pneumonia; div 2; number 6; with another; cost 2.

Feb 20; **Still born of W. Walker & wife**; still born; still born [cause of death]; div 2; number 206; with another; cost 2.

Feb 21; **Still born found dead on street** [NBN: "Entered as unknown"]; not given [gender]; still born [cause of death]; div 22; cost 0.

Feb 26; **Ora Roane Roane**; 22y; widow; phthisis pulmonalis; div 8; sec 4; cost 4.

Mar 2; **George Street** [Number next to name: "1260"]; 15y; single; ptomiania [?] poison; div 8; sec 3; cost 4.

Mar 13; **Tom Williams**; 1y; male; pthisis; div 2; number 97; with another; cost 2.

122 Richmond, Virginia, Mt. Olivet Cemetery Register

[1905 cont.]

Mar 25; **Florence Pugh**; 5y; female; whooping cough; div 2; number 105; with another; cost 2.

Mar 27; **America Mitchel**; 50y; widow; la guppee; div 17; sec 5; cost 4.

Mar 30; **Florence Faison**; 2m; female; inanition; div 2; number 39; with another; cost 2.

Apr 1; **Jas Perry**; 3m 12d; male; menengetis; div 1; cir 1; sec 18; cost 2.

Apr 7; **Thelma Jackson**; 1y; female; pneumonia; div 17; sec 5; cost 2.

Apr 7; **Cuffy Jasper Jr.**; 50y; married; enlarged prostrate; div 17; sec 4; cost 4.

Apr 11; **Elizabeth Sterling**; 24y; widow; phthisis pulmonalis; div 8; sec 1; cost 4.

Apr 13; **Eliza Lewis**; 3m 12d; single; hydrocephis; div 17; sec 1; cost 2.

Apr 22; **Lelia Pollard**; 5y; female; pertisisis; div 2; number 62; with another; cost 2.

Apr 22; **Chas Jefferson**; 32y; married; heart failure; div 1; cir 1; sec 21; cost 4.

May 1; **Rogoman Cheatham**; 9m; male; pneumonia; div 2; number 66; with another; cost 2.

May 8; **Gladys Powell**; 9m; female; bronchitis; div 22; order of mayor; cost 0.

Richmond, Virginia, Mt. Olivet Cemetery Register

[1905 cont.]

May 12; **Mary L. Smith**; 1y 4m; female; spinal menengetis; div 2; number 107; with another; cost 2.

May 15; **Lelia G. Seureoel [?]**; 47y; female; malaria; div 17; sec 4; cost 4.

May 19; **Catharine Taylor**; 62y; not given [marital status]; natural insufficiency; div 8; sec 1; cost 4.

May 21; **Thomas Dickinson**; 1y 8m; male; whooping cough; div 17; sec 6; cost 2.

May 29; **Peyton Quarles**; 50y; married; heart failure; div 1; cir 3; sec 1; cost 4.

Jun 11; **Infant of Wilson Crump**; 8m; male; gastro enteretis; div 2; number 194; with another; cost 2.

Jun 14; **Infant of Broaddus**; 9m; female; acute digestion; div 2; number 205; with another; cost 2.

Jun 23; **Hilda A Coleman**; 9m; female; meningetis; div 2; number 238; with another, cost 2.

Jun 25; **Persy Bailey**; 1y; male; entiretis; div 2; number 222; with another, cost 2.

Jun 25; **Thomas Sherron**; 18y; single; pneumonia; div 8; sec 3; cost 4.

[Page 36]

Jun 26; **Mary Dangerfield**; 47y; married; acute nephthritic; div 1; cir 1; sec 31; cost 4.

[1905 cont.]

Jun 26; **Roland Hickman**; 2y; male; menengetis; div 1; cir 1; sec 29; cost 2.

Jun 29; **Martha Meyo**; 6m; female; whopping cough; div 2; number 32; with another; cost 2.

Jul 3; **Dora Robinson**; 47y; married; heart disease; div 1; cir 1; sec 33; cost 4.

Jul 5; **Lee Roy Booker**; 1y 6m; male; pneumonia; div 2; number 82; with another; cost 2.

Jul 12; **Andrew Bailey**; 17y; single; burns; div 1; cir 1; sec 30; cost 4.

Jul 14; **Louisea Simmons**; 1y 6m; female; pneumonia; div 2; number 141; with another; cost 2.

Aug 4; **W. Y. Thompson**; 89y; widower; natural causes; div 17; sec 5; cost 4.

Aug 9; **Alversa Bailey**; 4m; male; menengetis; div 2; number 32; with another; cost 2.

Aug 11; **Wm Winfred**; 4y; male; malaria fever; div 1; cir 3; sec 68; cost 2.

Aug 12; **Moses Harris**; 52y; male; typhoid fever; div 1; cir 1; sec 35; cost 4.

Aug 12; **Zelina Logan**; 1y; female; cholera infantum; div 1; cir 1; sec 23; cost 2.

Aug 15; **Wm Brown**; 29y; single; consumption; div 8; sec 1; cost 4.

Richmond, Virginia, Mt. Olivet Cemetery Register

[1905 cont.]

Aug 23; **Hazle Bailey**; 1y 2m; female; cholera infantum; div 1; cir 1; sec 18; cost 2.

Sep 2; **Laura Robinson**; 56y; widow; heart disease; div 2; number 88; with another; cost 4.

Sep 13; **Robt P. Tilery**; 7m; male; cholera infantum; div 2; number 30; with another; cost 2.

Sep 15; **Jas. Robinson**; 2y; male; cholera infantum; div 17; sec 2; cost 2.

Sep 16; **Etta Bartlet**; 1y 3m; female; cholera infantum; div 2; number 67; with another; cost 2.

Sep 18; **Mary Davis**; 1y 6m; female; asthma; div 1; cir 3; sec 54; cost 2.

Sep 18; **Mary Harris**; 61y; not given [marital status]; nasal & gastris catarah [?]; div 8; sec 5; cost 4.

Sep 20; **Lawson Polk**; 50y; married; non contageous; div 17; sec 4; cost 4.

Sep 22; **Henry Johnson**; 2y 2m 4d; male; capilary bunc [?]; div 1; cir 3; sec 68; cost 2.

Sep 27; **Conrad Bacon Jr**; 29y; married; fracture skull; div 3; number 12; cost 4.

[Listing of costs stops at this point in the register.]

Oct 1; **Mariah Brooks**; 50y; married; pneumonia; div 1; cir 3; sec 1.

Oct 6; **Ruby Keys**; 3y; female; bronchal pneumonia; div 17; sec 6.

Richmond, Virginia, Mt. Olivet Cemetery Register

[1905 cont.]

Oct 9; **Willie Winston**; 1y; male; enteritis colotis; div 2; number 9; with another.

Oct 13; **Bettie Clarke**; 4m 12d; female; entero colotis; div 2; number 46; with another.

Oct 16; **Arthur Watson**; 6y; male; tonsilitis; div 1; cir 3; sec 54.

Oct 16; **Roach A. Pugh**; 2y; male; diarhoea; div 3; number 4; with another.

[Page 37]

Oct 24; **Frances Marshall**; 22d; female; entero colitis; div 2; number 29; with another.

Oct 24; **Infant of Henry Brooks**; male; still born; div 17; sec 4.

Oct 26; **Ony Jones**; 36y; married; tubercolosis; div 17; sec 6.

Oct 28; **Bennett Easeley**; 1y 4m 12d; tubercolosis; div 2; number 102; with another.

Nov 2; **Annie Pollard**; 23y; single; tubercolosis; div 2; number 93; with another.

Nov 11; **Allen Coles**; 41y; married; dysentery; div 1; sec 40.

Dec 5; **Blanche Allen**; 14y; single; endercarditis [?]; div 1; cir 1; sec 26.

Dec 17; **Julia Laws**; 26y; married; unknown [cause of death]; div 2; number 6; with another.

Dec 18; **Chas M. Henly**; 60y; married; heart disease; div 1; cir 1; sec 22.

[1905 cont.]

Dec 27; **Neal Harris**; 29y; married; pulmonary hemmorhague; div 17; sec 3.

Dec 30; **Langston Coles**; 41y; married; apoplexy; div 17; sec 1.

1906

Jan 8; **Mary Powell**; 69y; widow; nephthretis; div 1; cir 1; sec 36.

Jan 10; **Joseph Henry Robinson**; 10m 12d; male; pneumonia; div 2; number 93; with another.

Jan 17; **Robert H. James**; 65y; married; unknown [cause of death]; div 2; number 68; with another.

Jan 22; **Annie Deen** [NBN: "Entered as Deen & Dun"] 19y; single; pneumonia; div 1; cir 3; sec 64.

Feb 1; **Saml Booker**; 49y; widower; heart disease; div 2; number 84; with another.

Feb 2; **Jas. Royster**; 26y; married; pneumonia; div 1; cir 1; sec 18.

Feb 7; **Floyd Robinson**; 17y; single; pneumonia; div 1; cir 3; sec 64.

Feb 9; **Martha Paraham**; 59y; married; cancer of rectum; div 2; number 7; with another.

Feb 20; **Mary Williams**; 52y; married; nephthulis; div 17; sec 4.

Feb 26; **Earnest C. Munford**; 24y; single; tubercolosis; div 8; sec 3.

Mar 3; **Synthy Smith**; 65y; widower; apoplexy; div 2; number 228.

[1906 cont.]

Mar 11; **Dilsey Robertson**; 50y; widow; rheumatism; div 1; cir 1; sec 40.

Mar 12; **Sarah A Davis**; ? [age]; widow; carcinoma of breast; div 3; number 13.

Mar 17; **Mathews Wyatt**; 4y; male; broncho pneumonia; div 1; cir 1; sec 18.

Mar 19; **Infant of Jeff Coleman**; male; still born; div 1; cir 1; sec 18.

Mar 20; **John H. Love**; 54y about; married; Bright's disease; div 2; number 217; with another.

Mar 26; **Edwd Winston**; 41y; married; pneumonia; div 1; cir 1; sec 29.

[Page 38]

Apr 2; **Elsie Miller**; 29y; married; apoplexy; div 1; cir 1; sec 4.

Apr 6; **Susan Fife**; 65 or 70y; widow; heart disease; div 2; number 181; with another.

Apr 11; **Albert Mickens**; 45y; married; phthesis pulmonalis; div 1; cir 1; sec 33.

Apr 23; **A. S. Ballard**; 41y; not given [marital status]; pneumonia; div 17, sec 4.

Apr 27; **George Heart**; 60y; widow; congestion of lungs; div 2; number 64; with another.

May 7; **Mary Montague**; 2m 12d; female; unknown [cause of death]; div 3; number 13; with another.

[1906 cont.]

May 13; **Lavinia B. Deane**; 29y; married; typhoid fever; div 17; sec 5.

May 16; **Mamie Fields**; 17y; single; tuberculosis pulmonalis; div 1, cir 3; sec 54.

May 18; **Leroy Tinsley**; 1m 2d; male; infantile convulsions; div 1, cir 3; sec 68.

May 20; **Henry Reid**; 46y; single; acute gastritis; div 8; sec 1.

Jun 5; **Pecar[?] Hill**; 13y; male; tetanus; div 1; cir 1; sec 21.

Jun 12; **Henry A. Brooks**; 53y; married; ac. indigestion; div 1, cir 1, sec 27.

Jun 27; **Ellenora Chanler**; 15y; single; typhoid fever; div 8, sec 1.

Jun 28; **Hazel King**; ? [age]; male; unknown [cause of death]; div 2; number 20; with another.

Jul 6; **Priscilla Clarke**; 54y; married; acute gastritis; div 8; sec 1.

Jul 1[?]; **Matilda Trent**; 71y; married; apoplexy; div 1; sec 1; part of sec 40.

Jul 21; **Arthur Little**; 22y; single; heart disease; div 2; number 9; with another.

Jul 22; **Page Mosby** [NBN: "Entered as Mosby Page and Page Mosby"]; 7/12m[?]; male; natural; div 2, number 82; reopen.

Jul 24; **Inez Goode**; 20y 11m; single; div 1; cir 3, sec 68.

Jul 25; **Infant of Pinkee Jones** [NBN: "Entered as Pinkee Jone's infant"]; 9d; male; div 1; cir 1; sec 18.

[1906 cont.]

Aug 1; **G. R. Minus** [NBN: "Entered as Minus"]; 10m 12d; male; cholera infantum; div 2; number 4; reopen.

Aug 1; **Lotal Allen** [NBN: "Entered as Lotal"]; 2y; male; cholera infantum; div 8; sec 3.

Aug 4; **Grove Richardson** [NBN: "Entered as Grove"]; 7y 3m 25d; infantile convulsions; div 2; number 19.

Aug 4; **Infant of Geo Branch**; premature; premature [cause of death]; div 2; number 57; with another.

Aug 5; **Albert Henderson**; 41y; married; mine[?] [cause of death]; div 17; sec 5.

Aug 18; **Joe Diggs**; not given [age]; male; typhoid fever; div 22; number 369; order of Meyor.

Aug 18; **Infant of Willson Crump**; 1/12m[?]; female; whooping cough; div 17; sec 2.

Aug 18; **Benj Graham**; 1y; male; cholera infantum; div 2; number 80; with another.

Aug 22; **Minnie Lee Clarke**; 29y; married; hemorrhage; div 8; sec 6.

Aug 22; **Clara Waddele**; 21y; female; tuberculosis; div 2; number 68; with another.

Aug 25; **Helen Pride**; 13y; female; tuberculosis; div 1; sec 22.

Aug 30; **Leroy White**; 1y 4m; male; cholera infantum; div 2; number 79; with another.

Richmond, Virginia, Mt. Olivet Cemetery Register

[1906 cont.]

[Page 39]

Sep 1; **Lethia Williams**; 4y; female; measles; div 8; sec 4.

Sep 10; **Estelle Hobson**; 18y; single; ecclampsia; div 2; number 211; with mother.

Sep 11; **David Meekins**; 55; male; nephthritis; div 8; sec 1.

Sep 16; **Willie Clarke**; 1y; male; cholera infantum; div 2; number 20; with another.

Sep 24; **Nellie Hughes**; 37y; widow; apoplexy; div 1; cir 3; sec 68.

Sep 26; **Madeline Logan**; 4/12m[?]; female; cholera infantum; div 1; cir 1; sec 18.

Sep 26; **Lillie May Hobson**; 25y; single; nephthritis; div 1; cir 3; sec 54 [?]

Sep 28; **Willie Hobson**; 4m; acute nephritis; div 2; number 207; with another.

Sep 29; **Henry Davis**; 60y; nephthritis; div 1; cir 3; sec 16 [?].

Oct --; **Pelio Smith**; 21y; male; seasickness; div 1; cir 1; sec 19.

Oct 3; **Chas Moseley**; 8m; male; typhoid fever; div 2, number 49; with another.

Oct 8; **Norma Capers** [NBN: "Entered as Capers"]; 24y; married; accident; div 2; sec 32; with another.

Oct 10; **Edward Lee**; 26y; pneumonia; div 3; number 14.

132 Richmond, Virginia, Mt. Olivet Cemetery Register

[1906 cont.]

Oct 15; **Fred Rock**; 21y; male; tuberculosis; div 17; sec 4.

Oct 15; **Robert Flemming**; 46; appendicitis; div 1; cir 3; sec 64.

Oct 16; **Robert Moosley**; 69; apoplexy; div 2; number 22; with another.

Nov 6; **Jennie Byrd**; unknown [age]; female; tuberculosis; div 1; cir 1; sec 24.

Nov 6; **Curtis Talliferro**; 15y 9m; male; consumption; div 1; cir 1; sec 29.

Nov 9; **Ellenora Meyo**; 50y; female; paralysis; div 1; cir 1; sec 29.

Nov 10; **Louisa Jones**; 43y; female; phthisis; div 1; cir 1; sec 30.

Nov 18; **Infant of Wm Pleasants**; still born; still born [cause of death]; div 1; cir 1; sec 18.

Dec 3; **Roy De Witt Jackson**; 1m; male; marasmus; div 17; sec 1.

Dec 4; **Hellen Bland**; 1y; female; measles; div 2; number 3; with another.

Dec 16; **Mat Davis**; 95y; male; unknown [cause of death]; div 2; number 123.

Dec 19; **Charlotte Winfree**; 19y; female; tuberculusis; div 13; number 123[?]; with another.

Dec 24; **Edna Taylor**; 15y; single; tubercolosis; div 1; sec 33.

Richmond, Virginia, Mt. Olivet Cemetery Register

1907

Jan 8; **John Robinson**; 29y; rheumatism [?]; div 2; part of sec 16; with another.

Jan 11; **Sarah Feeney**; age [not given]; consumption; div 17; sec 4.

Jan 11; **Robert Russle**; 33y; tuberculosis; div 22; number 869 [?]; order of Meyor.

Jan 16; **Adeline Feeney**; 6m; bronchitis; div 17; sec 4.

Feb 4; **Robert Washington**; 38y; pneumonia; div 1; cir 3; sec 1.

Feb 5; **Fletcher Jackson**; 51y; not given [cause of death]; div 1; cir 1; sec 33.

Feb 8; **Maria Smith**; 38y; Bright's disease; div 2; number 5; with another.

Feb 9; **Howard Pleasants**; 4m; burns; div 2; number 12 [?]; with another.

Feb 11; **Willie Pollard**; 13y; Bright's disease; div 17; sec 4.

Feb 17; **Archer Taylor**; 38y; consumption; div 8; sec 3.

Feb 19; **Benj Jones**; 49y; hemorrhages; div 1; cir 1; sec 27.

[Page 40]

Mar 2; **Berta Stokes**; 63y; unknown [cause of death]; div 2; number 106; with another.

Mar 1; **Sarah Anderson** [NBN: "Entered as Andrews & Anderson"]; heart disease; div 1; cir 1; sec 23.

[1907 cont.]

Mar 1; **Nancy Jones**; 53y; div 1; cir 3; sec 68.

Mar 3; **Lucy Savage**; div 8; sec 2.

Mar 6; **Walter Flan** [NBN: "Entered as Flan"]; 2m; pneumonia; div 2; number 26 [?]; with another.

Mar --; **Louisa Howard**; 42y; apoplexy; div 17; sec 1.

Mar --; **C. L. Waller**; 4m; pneumonia; div 2; number 27; with another.

Mar 25; **Alex Johnson**; 55y; heart disease; div 1, cir 1, sec 32.

Mar 25; **Annie Gorden**; 38y; phthisis; div 2; number 107; with another.

Mar 30; **John P. Harris**; 34y; apoplexy; div 17; sec 4.

Apr 4; **Joe Edmons**; 52y; acute nephritis; div 1; cir 1; sec 17.

Apr 4; **Jas Jones**; 22y; pneumonia; div 2; number 43[?]; with another.

Apr 6; **May Foster**; 14y; tuberculosis; div 1; cir 1; sec 29.

Apr 7; **Sallie White**; 57y; heart disease; div 8; sec 5.

Apr 9; **Chas Harris** [NBN: "Entered as Hanes & Harris"]; 28y; Bright's disease; div 2; number 107.

Apr 11; **Robie Logan**; 9m; pneumonia; div 17; sec 3.

Apr 13; **Royall Smith**; convulsions; sec 2; number 82; with another.

Richmond, Virginia, Mt. Olivet Cemetery Register

[1907 cont.]

Apr 8 [?]; **Infant of Edmons**; still born; sec 2; number 89; with another.

Apr 17; **Bessie Scott**; 24y; maramus; div 1; cir 1; sec 30.

["13076" written lightly underneath "Bessie Scott."]

[Page 41]

May 2; **Annie L. James**; 44 or 50y; female; single; pneumonia.

May 4; **Fred Robinson**; 54y; male; married; gastritis.

May 7; **Robert Fowlkes**; 45 or 50y; male; married; pumonia.

May 19; **Mary Martin**; 51y; female; widower; pumonia.

May 20; **Martha Montague**; 18d; inamation; div 2.

May 20; **Bernard Lee Finney**; 11y; male; bronchitis.

May 22; **Robt Johnson**; 19y; male; pumonia.

May 23; **Elizabeth Baugh**; 17y; female; pumonia.

May 31; **William Brooks**; 7d; male; div 1; cir 1; sec 1; part of sec G.

Jun 8; **Henry Mason**; 65y; male; widow; apoplexy; div 1, cir 1; sec 40.

[Note: the register skips from June 8, 1907 to October 12, 1907. This gap takes place after the May 28, 1907 Manchester City Council meeting and the May 29, 1907 Manchester Cemetery Committee meeting regarding the cemetery superintendent's resignation and resulting approval to conduct an investigation. Refer to the Introduction for an explanation.]

[1907 cont.]

Oct 12; **Souissa [?] Howlett**; 23y; female; married; consumption; div 1; cir 3; sec 31; part of section Z.

Oct 12; **David Robinson**; 4m; male; consumption; div 1; cir 3; sec 35; part of section Z.

Oct 12; **Isabella F. Edmonds**; 28y; female; married; tubestruct [?] obstruction; div 1; cir 3; sec 29; part of sec Z.

Oct 24; **Robert Morton**; 8y; male; puemonia; div 1; cir 1; sec 1; part of sec G.

Oct 28; **Rebecca L Binga**; 56y; female; married; strangulated hernia; div 1; cir 1; sec 1; part of sec Z.

[Note: the register skips from October 28, 1907 to December 9, 1907.]

Dec 9; **Elizabeth B. Hill**; 23y; female; married; peumonia; div 1; cir 3; sec 41; part of sec T [?].

Dec 22; **Alton Hill**; 2m 8d; male; single; unknown [cause of death]; div 1; cir 3; sec 41; part of sec Y.

[Note: the register skips from December 22, 1907 to February 12, 1908.]

1908

Feb 12; **John H. Logan Jr.**; male; single; stillborn [cause of death]; div 1; cir 1; sec 27.

Richmond, Virginia, Mt. Olivet Cemetery Register

[1908 cont.]

Feb 13; **Henry Blackwell**; 77y; male; widower; senility; laborer; div 17; sec 1.

Feb 14; **Henry Spence Mason**; 5m 12 d; male; single; pneumonia; div 1; cir 1; sec 40.

Mar 7; **Lizzie Allen**; 85y; female; widow; gastritis; domestic; div 1; cir 3; sec 43; part of sec Y.

Apr 9; **Margurette M. Robinson**; 8m; female; broncho pneumonia; div 1; cir 1; sec 2; part of sec X.

May 4; **Cashett Baugh**; 1y 4m; female; single; cholera infantum; div 1; cir 3; sec 41; part of sec Y.

Jun 19; **Wilson Howlett**; 80y; male; widower; catorhal pneumonia; div 1; cir 6; sec 33; part of sec Z.

July 25; **Robt Goode**; 37y; male; single; nophritis; laborer; div 8; sec 4; part of sec V.

Aug 4; **Irly Robinson**; female; single; pneumonia; domestic; div 1; cir 3; sec 35; part of sec Z.

Sept 23; **Linwood Robinson**; 21y; male; single; tuberculosis; laborer; div 1; cir 1; sec 2; part of sec X.

Oct 5; **Ora. B. Skipwith**; 16y; female; single; tuberculosis; domestic; div 1; cir 1; sec 5; part of sec X.

Oct 28; **Martha Woolridge**; 67y; female; widow; chronic diarhea; house keeper; div 8; sec 4; part of sec V.

Nov 2; **Mason Baugh**; 16y 8m; male; single; pleuracy; laborer; div 1; cir 3; sec 41; part of sec Y.

138   Richmond, Virginia, Mt. Olivet Cemetery Register

[November 2, 1908 was the last interment entry; however the register contained 154 more pages that could have been used for entries. It was not researched why this register's use ended.]

[Loose letter was inserted into register, found on page 148, printed on letterhead:]

S. J. Jones, Superintendent

                Office of Superintendent,
                Maury and Mount Olivet Cemeteries.
                           Richmond, Va. _____ 191-

[Handwritten on letter:]

J. W. Wakefield, 214 E 6th St.
L. E. Booth, 1007 Decatur St.
C. H. Chalkley

APPENDIX

Speech of the Mayor of Manchester in 1878[1]

On March 13, 1878 the Mayor of Manchester, the Honorable Jas A Clarke, addressed the Manchester City Council during their regular meeting in the Council Chamber at 7 ½ O'clock PM. Note the comments about the cemetery's lack of section markers.

Accurate transcription of the minutes (including misspellings) has been attempted, yet is not guaranteed.

[Minutes start on page 260]

Mayors Office
Manchester March 13, 1878

To the City Council
                Gentlimen
                        Your Auditor and Treasurer having made their annual reports, and another fiscal year being commenced I proceed to Communicate to your honorable body as required by the Charter a general statement of the condition of the City in relation to its government finances and improvements. In as much as the Mayor has no voice and but little influence in the deliberation of the Council, with no power to forbid, nor even the privelege of gracefully approving its action it may well be asked why this particular provision was inserted in the charter, embracing as it does, every subject which can Concern the interest of the City. Such a communication would necessarily be a mear recapitulation of what the Council itself has done the details of which must be now familiar to every member of your body, than to any officer of the City. This provision of the charter, was however, no doubt intended to make it the duty of the Mayor to make such Suggestions or recommendations to the Council as in his opinion affected the public interest, and when made having of themselves no binding force, the council were at liberty to adopt or reject at their pleasure And the clause of the charter, adding nothing to the powers of the Mayor imposes upon him a very Serious responcibililty, and a duty the neglect of which might subject him to the anina divisions of a Court, the presentment of a grand Jury and a formal trial by the country, All of which I Suppose I have escaped in consequence of having been too young in office, To have incurred the penalties of disobedience, the clause of the charter to which I refer requires the clerk immediately after the close of each sesion of the [page 261] Council to make and present to the Mayor a transcript of every ordinance resolations & order concerning any public improvement, and for the payment of

Money, and every ordinance resolution, order and act of a legislative character pased by the City Council at such Sesion; immediately upon entering the duties of my office I Called the attention of the clerk to this Section of the charter, and this duty has been in every instance promptly complied with on his part, the charter however does not provide, or direct what the Mayor shall do with this transcript whe[n] he receives it, yet as it was no doubt inserted for some useful and proper purpose, it is fair to presume that it was intended that if in his judgment any ordinance of the Council should be considered Contrary to the general laws of the land a violation of the charter or unwise hasty and ill considered he should communicate such opinion to the Council which if he failed or neglected to do might subject him to prosecution for gross neglect of duty, and I am please here to say that so far I have seen no cause to complain of the proceedings of your body, but believe you have acted wisely and at all times strictly within the legitimate sphere of your duties. Your finances and the improvments of the streets and other public works are so intimately blended the one with the other that they cannot will be seperated, my predesosor in office in his first annual mesage made when the City was scarce sisc months old, speaks of the embarrased condition of the finances of the City, inherited from the board of Trustees, bonds unsaleable, & the interest of those sold unprovided for, the credit of the City generally damaged and justly congratulated in so short a time you had brought order out of chios, and restored the credit of the City. Now comes it then; that now after four years with a largely increased population, with the erection of so many and valuable private residences and other buildings, swilling the revenue from new subjects of Tascation why is it that the city instead of having shaken off this incubus of debt, or so diminishing it as make it lightly born, why has it now become a grave question how to meet the liabilities of the city without resorting to that last escpedient the ultimarates[?] of councils as well as of Kings, Tascation, but it is admitted that we have already reached the "Ultima Tule[?]" and can go no further, I am confident that you will readily find means to avoid such a necessity, which I am equally confident that in such an extremity a choice between tascation and dishonor, neither the Council nor the Citizens would hesitate to choose the first, we could not if would shelter ourselves behind an egnorminious repudiation, or forced terms of adjustment or readjustment with our creditors: I am confident that if we incur no more important and costly outlays in future we can safely and succesfully grapple with all our present difficulties and embarrasmints and laugh to scorn the idle mutterings of those who wish, and predict Receivership Bankruptcy and ruin to the City. From the report of your Treasurer I think we have reason of congratulations than cause of dissatisfaction, any inequity between Receipts and escpenditures being only tempoary and several instances accidental, the improvement upon the water line which are now competed have been unusually heavy the cost of building the new dam is stated to be [page 262] $7558.90 this work is however a permanant improvement, and will not inter into our future annual escpenditures. This sum of itself would be equal to the interest of on third of the whole bonded debt of the City which our resourses at the same time and from the same cause have been diminished, by the suspension of the Iron works and the Corn mill to which also may be added as an accidental escpenditure of $1325 paid to the County of Chesterfield on settlement on account of the Court House. Another considerable item of revenue has been almost entirely cut off during many months by the failure of the Hydrants rent the receipts from which are stated in the Treasurers Report to have been only $79 this rent I suppose will be very materially increased during the present year I am informed that the Hydrants rents are very partially and irregularly made and I suggest that the ordinances in relation to Hydrants be more strictly enforced, and the rent, now promptly Collected, and this can alwayes be done more easily than the collection of any other Tasc as the remidy is in the hands of the proper officers by simply cutting off the water upon nonpayment of the rent.

In relation to the cost of the present dam I am assured by your City Engineer that it has cost no more than it would have cost if built originally upon the same foundation and upon the same plan as it now stands, and he refers me to statistical statement filed by him with the Auditor, which I have not examined, but from his escplanations made to me I have no doubt will be substantial and to which I particularly call your attention great credit is due to the Engineer and the Committee under whose construction and vigelunt supervision this work has progresed to completion, and to the contractor for the rapidity and apparent solidity of the structure and the general faithful performance of his contract.

In regard to the water power of the City while I am aware of its great intrinsic value, I have never looked upon it as property, which could bring so much money directly unto the treasury but rather as the means whereby the wealth trade and population of the City would be immediately inescused, the greater portion of this property lies idle and unproductive yealding nothing and until utilised is of no more value than if we did not own it the only means then of making this power an addition to our Cash Capital or our annual revenue, is either by sale of the entire subject, or effecting new leases, which would of course bring new Capital and new population which would be new subjects of Tascation, equalling and perhaps esceeding in no great length of time, our whole present rivenue, and I would therefore desire to impress upon you this view of the subject to neglect no reasonable proposition for its purchase, but estimating in such sale the indirect and ulterior advantages that it would bring to our City – and in order to effect a fair sale or new leases great inducements should be held out to those desiring to become purchasers or lesees; From enquiries lately made by me at one of the mills on the waters rents, I was greatly supprized to be told, that the water line at Lowell[?] and other places, north were greatly below those paid here. I had always been of a very different impression, I donot [page 263] know however that there are not other compensating advantages in our favor, I have deemed it proper to call this question to your attention as one if I am correctly informed, deserving further enquiry and action while upon the subject of the River rights of the City I would respectfully direct your attention to a matter which I deem of great importance to the City. I have only heard within the last few days that the City of Richmond claims and escercises the right to collect the wharfage and other dues upon vessels loading and unloading cargoes on the southern shore of the River if these dues are so Collected for the use of the City of Richmond, if they had the legal right, I should regard it as, an unriasonable monopoly of the river, or manifest wrong to our city and the counties lying upon the southern side of the river, I have had no time to escamine fully into this question but from the slight and hasty escamination, which I have made the statues bearing upon the relative rights of the two Cities I can find no good grounds for this claim upon the part of the City of Richmond, but in as much as I suppose Manchester May not have been declared a port of entry having no Custom officers, all vesels trading here would clear from and to Richmond in cases of foreign vesels duties would very properly be collected by the officers of the general government, but as in the coasting trade there are no duties nor wharfage dues to the government it must be charges such as these which have been paid to the City of Richmond, and have been levied in one week only on as many as eighteen vesels, I may be in error in this matter, but as at present advised I think this question Should be closely looked into, and our rights promptly and energetically vindicated by the Courts or before the legislature, I understand however (although I have not seen a Copy of this bill) that an act of the present Legislature (which is now a law) has been prepared esctending the corporate limits to the river, it is presumed that this assumed right on the part of Richmond has been carefully guarded against.

I have always been a sincear advocate for the acquisition of Mayo's Bridge or building another along side of it as we have been authorized to do by an act of the General Assembly and I am now the more emphatically in favour of its purchase since the erection of the Free Bridge. I am clearly of opinion that the City whenever it could be done should have control of both bridges, to be free or not free, as might seem to conduce to the best interest of the City. I regard the building of this free bridge at the time it was built as unwise. I clearly foresaw that all the promises which had been predicted, would be falsified and that the City would have to meet its share of the interest upon its cost, and the annual escpenditure of keeping it in repair. I had no faith in the practical workings of the scheme among the other means of promise the necessary amount of Capital it was confidently asserted that the land owners of Chesterfield and the surrounding counties, for the right of perpetual free crossing, would subscribe liberally to the Capital stock, the privilege to be appurtenant[?] to the land thereby facilitating its sale, and increasing its value, & a far greater increase in the value of City property would be surely secured – Has property greatly increased in Town or County? [H]ave the land holders subscribed [page 264] largely to the capitol stock, on the contrary do we now find some of those large our side landed proprietors who were so confidently depended upon for a liberal subscriptions, actually appearing before Committees of the legislatures hotly opposing the pasage of the bill for purchasing Mayos Bridge.

I am gratified their efforts have been in vain and I trust the voters of Manchester will sanction the rights to purchase and that if this bridge half built with their own money the interest of which they have to pay shall be continued a free bridge to themselves, they are not bound to furnish a free pasage acros the river at their own escpense, free trade and free intercourse with our neighbors and even with other nations is a thing truly to be wished and should never to discouraged when there are reciprocal benefits conferred and received, but where, as in this case, all the advantagis are upon one side and none on the other, presents a case where we should decline to become the unselfish benefactor.

In relation to the improvments of the streets it seems to me that however much it might add to the comfort, the convenience of the citizens or the supposed adornment of the City, it was too great a work to have been undertaken or esceucuted as an entire job, too great a burthen to be borne all at once, whether to be paid for outright or the interest of the out lay to be provided for by Tascation. I think it would be difficult to find a parallel case, where a town which had escisted for over one hundred years suddenly enlarging its Corporate limits including an esctent of territory equal to its original boundaries, should undertake at a single bound with one mighty effort to grade & pave its whole esctent of Streets and side walks, an improvment of this magnitude is the slow groth of time, impropeble improvments will surely come with increased commerce and population and the requisit cost be distributed equally and annually out of accruing resources, and thus be lightly felt leaving no troublesome debt behind; We have no Railroads or canals terminating in our Town, there is no depot here or merchant mart for any of the Staple products of the Country and however much we may level, grade or pave our Streets, these will not bring of themselves new trade or population, our only wealth is in our Water power, and all our efforts should be directed towards securing from it all possible advantages. However bold may have been the conception of this universal inprovments of the streets, I think escperience has proved that it was a measure imprudent and unwise in the then condition of the public indebtednes, there are some men, and some measures when made which are as too far ahead of the times, as there are others too far behind, these improvments I think belong to the first and perhaps I may belong to the second, it strikes me possibly that with the completion of the improvments on 7th and 12th Streets north of Hull, these improvments should be instantly suspended. I would strongly recommend that beyond this esctent, not another bond be sold until our finances are in a more healthy condition, and they can be resumed with safety and propriety.

In the late grading escavation of the Streets basing the starting [page 265] point upon some line claimed to have been indicated by the original survey or Watkins Map, it has inevitably happened that these lines has been interrupted by buildings standing in the supposed Street, now if these improvments had been knowingly and wilfully put there or at a time when the lines of the streets were well known or could easily be shown by application to some public officer authorized to make them out, the sufferers would have no just cause to complain if they were required to remove them, but when it can be proved or is admitted that some of these buliding are more than 100 years old, and probably in some instances rected prior to the establishment of the town itself, when the Successive proprietors have continued all that time to pay the Tasces asesed upon them, and no threat until now that they would be required to remove them, or in case of their failure so to do they would be so removed at this escpense of the owners, thereby causing great damage and in some cases irremediable los. It seems to me that some amelioration of the severity of such a measure should have been made in cases of peculiar hardship it would certainly be more equatable in such cases to have adopted some system of partial compensation at least, and have avoided the resentment and indignation of the owners, and drive them to suits at law against the City, to defend which, may cost the City more than it would have done to have effected some fair & Satisfactory settlement or compromise with the owners of the property. It is true that one cause have been decided in the supreame Court of appeals in favor of the City, but it does not necessarily follow that every other case would be decided in the same manner, each case would depend upon its own particular merits. Several of these cases are now still pending, and the City should by no means neglect to defend them, a single verdict against the City might cost more than all of them could now be accommodated for upon just and honorable terms, in this matter I speak only of such obstruction in the streets as escisted prior to Percivals survey the parties erecting these buildings had their eyes open and built at their own risk. I would here add that in the case of Mayo Vs Murchie the judges speak as if Watkins' Map was before them, and in the late case of the Commonwealth Vs Taylor the papers in the case of Mayo Vs Murchie are mentioned as being lost or destroyed, which in fact these papers are at this moment in the Clerks' office of the Circuit Court of Chesterfield, and there is no such map in these papers, and if I remember rightly no reference to such in the whole record, at the same time I do find in these papers what may now be considered a literary curiosity a Copy of the Williamsburg Gazett of the date of 1768 containing the scheme of Byrds lottery I would therefore recommend, that the Council invite a conference with the owners whoes property may be damaged by the esctension of the streets where there is in an actual encroachment upon the streets and not a mere consequential damage, with a view to an amicable adjustment and compromise I think I can make this suggestion with perfect propriety as since my entrance into office, I have thought it would not be proper or becoming in me, to act as Counsel [page 266] in any suit against the City, having withdrawn from the cases where I had been employed, and in which I had received no fee nor escpected any, and therefore feel that I am disinterested in making the suggestions. I have lately and purposely visited Maury Cemetery, and am pleased to say that considering the small force employed the grounds seem to be remarkably neat and well kept, but I was surprised to be told by the superintendant that there was no plat of the grounds showing clearly and distinctly the location of each seperate section, it seems to me that this omission might hereafter lead to great confusion, as it often happens in locating graves in parts of the Cemetery not theretofore used, the superintendant is guided only by familiar knowledge of the grounds, a knowledge which it would be difficult to impart or to be acquired by a new or other officer, I was informed that a Surveyor had been at one time employed to do this particular work, and progressed so far as to make all necessary field notes and other preliminary materials, and that it would only required him about one month more additional work to have completed the survey and plat this surveyor was however suddenly arrested [stopped] in his work, and dismissed by the Committee or other proper authority on the score of economy as a useles escpenditure; the sections are now only marked by wooden pins which are too easily removed, and if removed difficult or impossible to be restored to their true places, these should be removed and replaced by boundary stones sus as used to mark the lots and streets of the City. I recommend that this work be at once resumed, and I presume that it could be done with les cost by employing the same engineer who has so much of the necessary material already prepared, and whose services can no doubt be again had while as these grounds. I incidentally noticed a fine bank of gravel, either a part of the main road or at least the property of the City, and was informed that the gravel was carted away just as it was dug from the banks to be used upon the road bed of the streets, and upon inquiry why it was not riddled[?] was told that this too had been forbidden, the superintendant stated that by actual trial that in every three cart loads, there were two loads of earth, and one of Stone, causing as I think a useles waste of time labor and escpense, in hauling from so distant a point, earth which if wanted, could be had from more convenient places, and depositing it upon the streets where it was not wanted, and where it would do more harm than good, I call the attention of the present cemetary committee to these matters as I believe they were not done under their directions. There still remains several other subjects of great interest to the City, which it may not be considered out of place to mention, which however in the present condition of the treasury it might not be prudent to carry out now, but which in my opinion are of primary importance, and should be undertaken at the first practicable opportunity. These are 1st an alms house and a work house, or both combined, and the one or the other or both might be made at least practically self supporting, it is almost an anomomaly in society that at this moment we haven not an adult [page 267] pauper in our city, although it is true we have two twin children provided for else where, at the public escpense, the total absence of pauperism in the City may be partly owing to the fact that there is not established refuge for the poor maintained at the public charge, only private benevolent asiciations, yet it would not do to boast that there was no poverty of destitution, such can hardly be the fact, and where it escist, it must be relieved by the hand of private charity, which speaks volums in behalf of the humianity of our people. There outside of the cemetery enclosure, twenty acres of land, the property of the City, which would furnish an eligible suite for the erection of buildings suitable for such purpose, and might be built at no great Cost and the annual escpenses of supporting the establishment not much greater than is now encurred in the support of the twins before mentioned and such paupers as we may reasonable calculate upon these seeking admision, and whom otherwise the City might have to provide for the duties of superintending the establishment and providing for the inmates might be emposed upon the superintendant of the cemetery who should receive a moderate addition therefor to his salary. 3rd. The City needs a jail, not a misnamed prison where the perpetrators of great crimes could be safely kept, and where petty thieves easily escape, and those who are well contented where they are perfer to remain located where it is it is a standing nuisance to the town, and a disgusting annoyace to the nieghbourhouse where the profanity of crime and the ravings of insanity reach even to the council chamber itself. A secure jail in a more proper and suitable place should be built, whenever the ability of the City consistent with other escpenditures, will permit it to be done.

4th. An ample and unfairly suply of water to the hydrants and fire plugs. My predesor very quaintly observes that the location of the present reservoir had even been a mystery. I can assure him that it still remains a mystery and one that is not probable be ever be solved surely there can be nothing of greater importance to a City than an abundant supply of water for all houshold uses and security against fire. During the long suspension of the improvment on the water line there was great and constant apprehension lest a conflagration might break out, and which might have laid the greater portion of the City in ashes, happily we have escaped this peril. This is a matter of vital importance, indeed of necessity, the present supply is wholly in sufficient and otherwise objectionable. The engine with its highest capacity can but supply water to one half of the town, is liable to frequent interruptions form breakages of the machinery, and other accidents a long the line of the Canal, and occasional high floods in the river, this mode of supply should be abandoned as soon as the resources of the City with justify, and a nother site which should be no mystery should be selected upon some sufficiently elevated point near the City, upon which should be erected the necessary buildings with a pump of sufficient forcesing power to lift the water directly from the river into a capacious reservoir, from which it could be distributed to all parts of the City. I will take the libity of making here a suggestion which occured to me during my visit to the cemetery grounds. I find here that the streams from three very bold springs are united [page 268] or could very easily be united these streams together would form a very considerable colum of water, and in the opinion of those much better able to advise upon the subject could be brought into the City at no very great cost, a large cistern or reservoir could be built in some eligible location in the upper part of the town which would supply that portion with good water for all purposes, and for the esctinguishment of fires. I mearly throw out this suggestion for such consideration as the Council may think it deserves.

5. As to the City lamps

This is par escellence the age of inventions and discovery and no subject has undergone more disensions and more escperiments than that of the best mode of lighting the streets, so many different illuminating oils and gasses are daily offered to the public each claiming greater superiorty the one over the other, that it has become quite a difficult matter which to choose for before one can be fairly tested, another is forced upon the attention, as of les cost or greater illuminating power, the present manner of lighting the city is complained of as too partial, the lamps are principally upon the main Street where they are the least necessary where the lights of the Stores and houses in the early[?] part of the evening give all the light that is required, and whenever in the darkest night the line of housed and the level pavment afford all necessary direction, while upon the remoter and les populous part of the town, where deep cuts and high embankments abound the lamps are few and far between, and gives but little ~~light~~ help to the pasing pedestrian; these lights are of course escpensive in material, and from the esctended circuit of the town must require at least two men to light and clean the lamps, who must be paid for their work, and you will soon have no police men who could be charged with that duty I have introduced this subject only to fill up the long catalogue of actual and contemplated retrenchment and reform and to add that if it be the pleasure of the Council to dispose with the lamps that no new substitute should be adopted without the closest escamination and comparison with all the different plans for lighting the streets of a City now in use–But For [illegible] lente[?] [illegible]ment, make haste slowly we are a City only four years old an infant corporation, and must yet weare the garment proper to infancy and not before our time asume the habiliments of manhood, all these much needed and much desired improvments, I have mentioned will all come in the due course of time we must look to the future for our growth and prosperity when Manchester becomes as it must do Known and ranked as a great Manufacturing

Town when her own Mills and factories shall bear their own distinct marks and b[illegible], and be recognized and esteemed in every part of the world, for their escellence, and not creep abroad and into foreign countries under a borrowed name. I take pleasure in commending to your most favorable consideration the several officers of the City, and especially to the members of the Police force, with whom I am daily more associated and can therefore speak more advisedly of their official conduct. In my intercourse with the various officers of the City, I have found them uniformly courteous, capable, diligent, [page 269] prompt, vigilant and faithfull in the discharge of their seperate duties, but I am constrained at the same time to say, that I much question the wisdom of the policy of the late action of the council in relation to the reduction of the salaries of these officers. I think this measure not demanded by the servises of the City or by the condition of the finances. I do not think it to be well considered economy; I feel the more free to speak upon this subject, as my own term of office is not effected by the proposed reduction and will escpire before it takes effect; surely four policemen, only two of whom can be on duty at a time, cannot be considered too many for a town now claiming a population over seven thousand, the additional duly lately required whereby one policeman is to be detailed daily to take charge of the chain gang virtually leaving on every other day, no policeman on duty as it is well known that so many and so important are the other duties of the chief of Police that it would be imposible for him to perform the ortinary duties of a Police officer, so that on these days the City is actually without any police officer at all. If the City could well afford the charge I would rather be disposed to see the police force increased than dimished in one breath the Council generously makes them a present and with the nesct with a prudent eye to frugality takes off perhaps twice the amount from their salaries. Oh consistency thou are a jewell; the pay of the officers of the City upon entering upon their duties was no doubt the chief inducement for accepting the offices, this pay was a sure certain and they naturally supposed that there would be some permanency in this pay and I do not think it altogether just or fair now that they have become familiar with their duties, to drive them to resignation or to continue to perform duties for salaries insufficient for their support these officers have had no past in bringing the City into debt, and yet they are the first to feel the heaviest force of the blade of Retrenchment and reform, if these be indispensable, let the blow fall upon the escpenditures themselves the public service can only be effectively performed by officers of skill, intregrity and ability and these qualifications should be carefully looked to in their selection, and a fair and reasonable compensation should be allowed them, sufficient for the decent subsistence of themselves and their families no doubt that other persons might be found who would undertake these officers at greatly reduced rates, and those who now hold them, if reelected or reappointed might continue to serve from sheer necessity and the uncertainty of finding new avocation, I do not consider it good policy to set up the offices of the City to the lowest bidder. In the office which I now hold by the favor of the Council, the Mayor of the City of seven thousand inhabitants is required to hold a police court every day to perform many other duties, his court must be opened at 9 Oclock every morning, he must be present every day it is commonly 10 or 11

Oclock before it closes, and in cases where many witnesses are escamined, and cros escamined, and the argument of Counsil heard, three or four hours are comsumed, what time would he have to attend any other regular buisnes requiring his personal attention, and for all this you propose to pay him eighty cents per day, by the original Charter this salary would be now $700–and you have now reduced this Salary to $300–considerably less than one half the power to do this has been given to you by an amindment to the Charter, why it was done I do not know, [page 270] certainly it was upon no complaint of the people, and still les upon the ground of retrenchment and reform. Besides I do not think this course is just and fair to the people themselves, who before making a choice, must first ascertain whether the individual they might prefer to be elected could afford to serve for the prescribed compensation, on such conditions the very best Citizens one whom the people might perfer over all other Citizens would be escluded, set aside and virtually disfranchised, the Mayor is supposed to be, and ought to be, a Citizen of good repute, intelligent, and from in his character and some what familiar with the law which he is called upon to administer, and should be fairly remunerated for his services.

I think I have good ground to congratulate you upon the unusual peace and good order privailing in the City, there has been as the proceeding of the Mayors Court will show, a marked decline in crime, and a total absence of all offnces of a high grade, in this respect I think our City may compare with if not escell any City in the Union of a equal population.

I am indebted to the Auditor and Treasurer for much Statisical information, which has been of great asistance to me in the preperation of this communication, and I regret to see that they have not escaped the keen edge of the knife of retrenchment and reform and should be pleased to see that you had reconsidered your action and their Salaries to their present amount, which I am satisfied they honestly earn and well deserve.

So far from the late judicial inquisition, and which was attended with considerable cost to the City being calculated to enqure its credit I think in connection with the Treasurers escpose of our finances, should have, and in ought to have a directly different effect, and has placed the Credit of the City on the firmest basis, resulting after the most unescamplid and vigorous probing into all our monetary affairs, and which is proved by actual sale of City bonds, which are not higher in the market than they have ever been, it is a matter well understood by the holders of our securities that whatever differences may escist among ourselves as to the undertaking of improvments either by completing old ones or providing for new ones that the first case of the Council has always been to set aside a sufficient amount to meet the interest of the bonded debt of the City. I am aware that in works of political economy, it is said that the lighest[?] securities are those of the government, but it is has been always a matter not clearly comprehended by me why investors of Money whose sole object is the interest, Should lend money to the government at a very low rate of interest say three or four per cent, and hesitate to invest in the bonds of a City, bearing more than double that interest, and having an equal time to run, and whose capacity to pay that interest is beyond all doubt or even surprised.

This investigation into our affairs has shown as I am escplicity infomed your attorney, that the City will not lose a single dollar, and more over resulted in the complete acquital of every member of your body for you were indited in Mas and with an entry upon the record that there was nothing in all the evidence to show that there was any cause to charge any member of the [page 271] Council with correct or willful neglect or gros inattention to their official duties. I had no idia gentlemen whin I commenced this communication of the esctent to which it would lead, I had no purpose of inflicting upon you the long and perhaps valueles paper, but so many are the subjects embraced in the con[illegible] language of the charter, requiring the Mayor to make to you, an annual mesage, that I did not know to make it les.

In conclusion gentlemen I beg leave to say in justice to myself, that never having before participated in the public affairs of the City having been so short a time in office that it could hardly be escpected that I should be intimatily acquainted with the mint of all questions touching the public service, and I shall therefore claim your indulgences for the many crudities of this communication, and having the highest respect for your Honorable body and the utmost confidence in your ability integrity and public spirit I am sure you will go on as you have hitherto done to conduct the public affairs of our City with a single view to its increase in wealth population and commerce I remain

                                        yr. obt. Srvt.
                                        Jas A Clarke Mayor

---

[1] Richmond (City), Manchester City Council Minutes Book 2, 1875–1880. Library of Virginia, Richmond. Reel 993.

BIBLIOGRAPHY

Public Records

Authors Unknown. *Maury (Whites in Maury) April 1874–December 1908.* [The interment ledger is located at the Maury/Mt. Olivet Cemetery Office in Richmond, Virginia.]

Authors Unknown. *MT. OLIVET (Colored in Maury) 1875–April 1907.* [The interment ledger is located at the Maury/Mt. Olivet Cemetery Office in Richmond, Virginia and actually contains interments through November 1908.]

City of Richmond, Virginia. Department of Recreation & Parks. Bureau of Cemeteries. "Unknowns." Maury Cemetery, Richmond, Va., November 1981.

Richmond (City) Clerk and Council Manchester, Maury Cemetery Minutes, 1907-1910. Library of Virginia, Richmond. Reel 1000.

Richmond (City), Manchester City Council Minute Book 2, 1875 1880, Library of Virginia, Richmond. Reel 993.

Richmond (City), Manchester City Council Minute Book 5, 1897–1909. Library of Virginia. Richmond. Reel 994.

Published Works

Davis, Veronica. *Here I Lay My Burdens Down.* Richmond, Va: Deitz Press, 2003.

Frantel, Nancy C. *Chesterfield County, Virginia Uncovered, the Records of Death and Slave Insurance Records for the Coal Mining Industry, 1810–1895.* Westminster, Md: Heritage Books, 2008.

152 Richmond, Virginia, Mt. Olivet Cemetery Register

Lutz, Francis Earle. *Chesterfield, An Old Virginia County Volume I, 1607–1954.* Richmond, Va. Bermuda Ruritan Club, 1954. Reprint, Chesterfield County Historical Society, 2003.

Weisiger III, Benjamin B. *Old Manchester & Its Environs, 1769–1910.* Richmond, Va. William Byrd Press, 1993.

Newspaper Articles

Richmond Enquirer. "INTERMENTS." Richmond, Va. August 17, 1874.

Richmond Enquirer. "THE TOWN CEMETERY." Richmond, Va. March 13, 1874.

INDEX

ABRAM
 Narh, 63
ACKERMAN
 Celia, 29
ADKINS
 Maria, 52
 Willie, 32
ALLEN
 Alfred, 73
 Blanche, 126
 Eliza I, 53
 Erminie, 91
 Eugene, 81
 Infant of Mary, 52
 Jno R, 58, 60
 Lena E, 61
 Lizzie, 137
 Lotal, 130
 Lottie Belle, 90
 Margaret, 107
 Mary, 58, 60
 Mathews, 111
 Rachael, 46
 Sadie C, 95
 Samuel, 58
 Sidney, 102
 Wilson, 28
AMBLER
 Lucy, 46
ANDERSON
 A J, 113
 James, 28
 Roberta, 83
 Sarah, 133
 Sarah Jane, 28
ANDREWS
 David, 72
 Martha, 78
 Melvina E, 102
 Sarah, 133
 Sydney, 70

ARCHER
 Henritta, 62
 Rubin, 90
ARMSTEAD
 Francis, 69
 Josephine, 57
 Lottie May, 110
 Nerah, 57
 Robert, 106
 Samuel, 61
ARMSTED
 Sally, 41
AUSTER
 Octavia, 74
AUSTIN
 Willis, 107
BACON
 Conrad, 103
 Conrad Jr, 125
 Margarette, 116
BAILEY
 Alice, 50
 Alversa, 124
 Andrew, 124
 Eliza, 101
 Hazle, 125
 Mary Ellen, 45
 Persy, 123
BAILIE
 Elishae, 59
BAKER
 Abner, 116
 Henry, 70
 Infant of Nannie, 85
 James, 69
 Martha, 40
 Mary E, 34, 94
 Mary M, 52
 Robert, 54
 Welthy Jane, 33

BALL
  Alice, 64
BALLARD T
  A S, 128
BANKS
  John, 29
  Martha, 37
  Nancy, 53
BARBELL
  Stephen, 47
BARCROFF
  L H, 41
BARKSDALE
  George, 90
  Robert, 87
BARNES
  Mike, 99
BARTLET
  Etta, 125
BAUGH
  Albert, 56
  Cashett, 137
  Douglass, 38
  Elisabeth, 25
  Elizabeth, 26, 40, 135
  Jas A, 111
  Julia, 35, 57
  Julia Ann, 104
  Mason, 137
  Mildred, 42
  Mollie, 51
  Sarah, 41
  Stephen, 36
BELL
  Mary, 25
BENNETT
  Edna, 68
BENTLEY
  Doctor, 65
BERRYMAN
  Wm, 68
BINGA
  Anthony Sr, 98
  Rebecca L, 136
  Rhoda, 49

BIRD
  Richard, 61
BLACKWELL
  Elizabeth, 106
  Henry, 137
  James W, 43
BLAKLEY
  Joe, 110
BLAND
  Cornelia, 31
  Harvey O, 41
  Hellen, 132
  Henry, 37
BOCK
  Fannie, 105
BOLLING
  Matilda, 33
BOLLINGS
  Maria, 111
BOOKER
  Blanche, 111
  Easter, 48, 51
  Harriette, 71
  Infant of Saml and Laura, 102
  Infant of Wanda, 42
  Infant of Wm and wife, 90
  Joseph, 34
  Lee Roy, 124
  Luther, 50
  Mary, 48, 51, 89
  Mary F, 60
  Russell, 63
  Saml, 127
  Willie, 45
BOOTH
  L E, 138
BOTTS
  James, 67
BOWEN
  Bessie, 110
BOWMAN
  Lewis, 88
BOYD, 37
  Infant of Eliza, 35
  Sally, 108

BRADLEY
  Edward, 115
BRADSHAW
  Infant of Kate, 80
  Kate, 80
BRANCH
  Eddie, 52
  Fred, 119
  Infant of Geo, 130
  Infant of Richard, 100
  Infant of Robt, 119
  J M, 76
  Lena, 78
  Mandy, 50
  Mary H, 53
  Roswell, 121
  Wm, 119
  Woodson, 55
BRANCHE
  Blanche, 51
BRICE
  Williams, 87
BRIGGE
  Adam, 85
  London, 48
BRIGGS
  Alexander, 41
  Amey, 48
  Peter M, 117
BRIGHT
  Elizabeth, 100
  Squire, 86
BRINTON
  Rebecca, 85
BRITTON
  Blanche, 118
BROADDUS
  Infant of, 123
BROKIS
  Infant of Sam and Wife, 70
BROMSKILL
  Wesley, 71
BROOKS
  Ada, 92
  Alma Lee, 112

BROOKS (cont.)
  Henry A, 129
  Hilton Jr, 47
  Infant of Henry, 126
  John, 52
  Joseph, 97
  Louisa, 89
  Lucie M, 39
  Lucy, 101
  Mariah, 125
  Mrs Mary, 39
  Otis, 91
  Patsey, 27
  Sam'l, 99
  Stepen, 93
  William, 135
  Wm D, 55
BROWN
  Alice, 108
  Augustus, 106
  Elizabeth, 102
  Frances, 53
  George, 79
  Henry, 112
  Infant of M and M, 61
  J M, 94
  James, 35
  John, 117
  Lou B, 55
  Wm, 124
BRUCE
  Fanny, 58
  Wm, 79
BULLOCK
  Millie, 110
BUNDY
  John, 113
BURFOOT
  Arthur, 75
  Florence C, 29
  Lizzie, 28
  Mary, 40
  Mat, 42

156 Richmond, Virginia, Mt. Olivet Cemetery Register

BURFORD
  Carrie, 46
  Marcus, 77
BURFURD
  Ella W, 43
BURK
  Thomas, 28
BURKE
  Maria, 46
  Volley, 77
BURKS
  Wise, 120
BURNETT
  Dixin, 75
BURRELL
  Henry, 59
BURTON
  Bessie, 79
  Paulina, 55
BURWELL
  Anderson, 26
  Parthemia, 26
BUSBY
  Jas, 95
BUSH
  Rebeccah, 53
BYRD
  Jennie, 132
C
  Jack, 76
CABBELL
  Matte, 56
CABELL
  Sarah, 71
CAPERS
  Norma, 131
CARINGTON
  Wm, 105
CARMPTON
  Rebecca, 60
CARRINGTON
  Ed Paul, 62
  Infant of Mary L, 103

CARTER
  Child of Laura, 66
  Eliza, 45
  Infant of Payton, 68
  Joseph H, 67
  Rachel, 70
  Robt, 27
CASSELL
  Lucy, 43
CEASAR
  Infant of R and wife, 81
CHALKLEY
  C H, 138
CHANDLER
  Georgie A, 65
  Roderick, 39
CHANLER
  Ellenora, 129
CHAPMAN
  Ananiss, 67
  Patrick, 63
CHATHAM
  Infant of Martha, 72
  Infant of Mary, 70
CHEATHAM
  Amy, 34
  Anica, 30
  Rogoman, 122
CHRISTIAN, 46
  Anna, 56
  Lucy, 101
  Mary, 73
  Nathaniel, 94
  Walter, 34
  Wm, 105
CHRISTMAS
  Effie, 116
CLAIBORNE
  Augustus, 69
  Jane, 32
CLAIRBORNE
  Welton, 55
CLARK
  Mary E, 25
  Nancy, 26

Richmond, Virginia, Mt. Olivet Cemetery Register

CLARKE
   Bettie, 126
   Jas A, 139
   Lewis H, 52
   Minnie Lee, 130
   Nancy, 27
   Priscilla, 129
   Willie, 131
CLAY
   J H, 51
CLAYBORNE
   Martha Ann, 54
COATES
   Virginia, 96
COLE
   Infant of Bettie, 29
COLEMAN
   Algie Davis, 102
   Ann, 30
   Annie B, 107
   Davie, 80
   George, 87
   Hilda A, 123
   Infant of Allen, 83
   Infant of J and L, 114
   Infant of Jeff, 128
   Jas, 39
   Mary, 113
   Nelson, 82
   Susan, 36
COLES
   Allen, 126
   John, 59
   Langston, 127
   Mary Jane, 105
COLIMA, 64
COLIS
   Marian, 100
COLMAN
   Rosa, 78
COOK
   Earnest, 59
   Infant of Mary J, 89
COOPER
   Jas Washington, 82

COPELAND
   Algie, 100
   John H, 81
CORMYTON, 64
CORRINGTON
   Millie, 66
COSELEY
   Hattie, 61
COX
   Joe, 35
   Sally, 77
COY
   Ellen E, 77
   Infant of David and wife, 96
   Infant of David I and wife, 94
   J H, 76
   S Arthur, 52
   Viola, 46
CRAMPTON
   Sallie, 112
CREAR
   Mary, 99
CRUMP
   Amanda, 91
   Infant of Willson, 130
   Infant of Wilson, 123
CUNNINGHAM
   Elizabeth, 109
   Florence A, 31
   Henry, 75
   Infant of Eliza, 105
   Parthenia, 97
CURTTNEY
   Henry, 80
DABNEY
   George, 102
   Joseph, 75
DANCEY
   Bruce, 114
   Clarence, 115
DANDRIDGE
   Henry, 47
   Kate, 41
DANGERFIELD
   Mary, 123

DAVIES
  Emily, 25
DAVIS, 65
  Alexander, 59
  Edward, 42
  Henry, 49, 131
  John, 121
  Malinda, 47
  Mary, 125
  Mat, 132
  Pearl, 121
  Rosa, 107
  Sarah Anne, 128
DEAN
  Abner, 27
  Edward, 43
DEANE
  Carrie, 92
  Lavinia B, 129
  Maria, 115
DEEN
  Annie, 127
DEJUSTO
  Carter G, 44
DENNIS
  Archer, 39
  Betsy, 62
  John, 81
  Wm D, 66
DICKENSON
  Jos, 40
DICKERSON
  Milley, 45
DICKINSON
  Thomas, 123
DIGGS
  Joe, 130
DIXON
  Susan, 25
DODSON
  Wyatt, 100
DOZELLE
  Mary, 96
DRAKE
  Jas, 96

DUN
  Annie, 127
DUNN
  Jas, 113
EASELEY
  Bennett, 126
EASTERS
  Alice, 77
EATON
  Infant of Jno and wife, 98
  John H, 92
EDGE
  George, 69
EDLOE
  Henry, 115
EDMONDS
  Isabella F, 136
EDMONS
  Cora, 104
  Henrietta, 115
  Infant, 135
  Infant of Mary, 110
  Joe, 134
EDMONSON
  Vernon L, 116
EDMUNS
  Infant of Ema, 95
EDWARDS
  Ballard T, 37
  Ethel T, 49
  Infant of Lena, 85
  Lena E, 55
  Mary, 44
EGGLESTON
  Jno, 95
ELLEOTT
  Merchant, 55
EPPS
  Martha, 54
  Mary, 54
ERWIN
  Ida C, 63
FAISON
  Florence, 122

FEENEY
  Adeline, 133
  Sarah, 133
FERGERSON
  John Henry, 77
FERGUSSON
  Curtis, 106
FIELDS
  Florence W, 80
  Isham, 74
  James A, 72
  Mamie, 129
  Martha J, 73
FIFE
  Florence, 53
  Herman, 70
  J H, 53
  Susan, 128
FINEY
  Mary Jane, 32
FINNEY
  Annie, 117
  Antelia, 45
  Bernard Lee, 135
  Charlie, 62
  Cornelius, 93
  Jas, 63
FINNIE
  Annie, 87
FINNIR
  Joseph, 75
FITZ
  Carrie L, 103
  Jas T, 116
FITZGERALD
  Catharine, 107
  Ella, 49, 61
  Margaret, 49
  Margarette, 61
FLAN
  Walter, 134
FLEMING
  Bessie, 25
  Garnett Wm, 104
  Lewis, 38

FLEMMING
  Emmit, 108
  Fanny, 67
  Mary, 37
  Robert, 132
  Sam'l, 62
  Willie, 31
FLOURNOY
  Bosher, 76
FORD
  Child of N L, 80
FORTUNE
  George, 83
FOSTER
  Anna, 54
  Benjiman, 57
  Cary, 96
  F Lee, 91
  Horace, 84
  Jas, 108
  May, 134
  Mrs Fannie, 67
FOUNTAIN
  Geo W, 92
  Infant of J and M, 53
  Susie B, 117
FOWLER
  Harvey, 81
FOWLKES
  Norma, 50
  Richard, 112
  Robert, 135
FREEMAN
  Infant of Wm H, 101
  Mary, 82
  Mary E, 101
FRIEND
  Georgie, 52
FUINOR
  Joseph, 75
FURGERSON
  Elvira, 97
  Fannie, 80
  Infant of Major, 98

GAINES
  Patsy, 66
GAINS
  Mary E, 41
GARLAND
  Edward, 90
GARNETT
  Robert, 96
GARRATE
  Wesley, 36
GARY
  Johnson, 98
GIBSON
  Hannah, 53
  Immanuel, 120
  Infant of Mary, 81, 83
  James, 86
  Mary, 79
  Thomas, 65
  Thos, 40
GILES
  Alex, 37
  Paulina, 37
  Sidney E, 120
  W H, 102
  Wm, 67
GILL
  Josephine, 73
GIPSON
  Child of Alice, 64
  Cora Lee, 120
GISONI
  Wm, 65
GIZZARD
  Isaac, 58
GLASGOW
  Infant of Mary, 59
GLASSGOW
  Mollie, 59
GLENFORD
  Emanuel, 58
GOFF
  Jordan, 32
GOLDEN
  Kathleen, 93

GOODE
  Alice Belle, 65
  David, 116
  Eliza, 115
  Elizabeth, 64
  Eva, 37
  Inez, 129
  Infant of Bettie, 97, 104
  Infant of Jas, 26
  Infant of Joseph, 68
  Infant of Nettie, 110
  Infant of T and A, 112
  Infant of Wm and wife, 91
  Jas, 83
  Joseph, 56
  Julia, 32
  Laura, 53
  Rhoda, 42
  Robt, 137
GOONELE
  Jas, 94
GORDEN
  Annie, 134
  Jas, 81
GORDON
  Lee, 103
  Lelia Isabelle, 116
GRAHAM
  Aley H, 92
  Benj, 130
  Florence, 112
  Lucy I, 64
GRAVES
  Ceasar, 38
  Czar, 36
GRAY
  George, 98
  Infant twins of Henry M(?)free
    (Winfree) and Billie (Bettie)
    Gray, 117
  William, 56
GREEN
  Alex, 110
  Anna Bell, 37
  Betsy, 92

GREEN (cont.)
  Beverly, 76
  Effie S, 48
  Herbert R, 115
  Infant of Jas and wife, 108
  James, 76
  Littie, 75
  Nancy, 81
GREGORY
  Annettia, 75
  Susan, 52
GRIFFIN
  Adelaide, 74
GRIMM
  John, 117
GUTHRIE
  Charlott, 31
HACKNEY
  Floyd, 72
  Mary, 120
HADEN
  Emily, 76
  Jas, 106
HALL
  Eva B, 46
  Francis, 74
  Isaac, 54
  James, 94
  Lewis A, 121
  Lucy A, 43
  Spencer T, 110
HAMLIN
  Police, 116
HANES
  Chas, 134
HANKINS
  Infant of A and Wife, 87
  A J, 77, 88
  Matilda, 88
HARGROVE
  Geo, 106
HARRIS
  Adam, 117
  Adeline, 42
  C W, 88

HARRIS (cont.)
  Chas, 107, 134
  Coleman, 44
  Edward, 77
  Eli, 73
  Florence, 48
  George, 54
  Henrietta, 78
  Henry, 90
  Ida, 57
  Infant of Ellen, 31
  Infant of Henrietta, 78
  Infant of Robert and wife, 95, 104
  John P, 134
  Lizzie, 89, 101
  Lucy, 50
  Martha, 63
  Mary, 69, 125
  Mat, 66
  Moses, 124
  Nannie, 74
  Neal, 127
  Nellie, 109
  Preston, 86
  Robert W, 119
  Sallie, 88
  Susan, 65
HARRISS
  Elizabeth, 41
  Jennie, 33
HARVEY
  China, 107
  Nettie, 72
HASTINS
  Sam'l, 108
HATCHER
  Gladys, 107
  Jas, 95
  Sarah Anne, 70
HAWKINS
  Johnnie, 73
HAXALL
  Josephine, 29

HAXELL
    Infant of Sarah, 36
    Jas H, 113
HAYES
    Harvey, 70
    Hezekiah, 74
HAYS
    Ellen, 101
    Mary, 38
HEART
    George, 128
HEATH
    Infant of Hattie, 38
HEIGHT
    Infant of jas and M, 109
    Mrs Martha, 109
HENCE
    Infant of Mary, 110
HENDERSON
    Albert, 130
    Eugine, 44
    H L, 58
    Hannibal, 75, 84
    Louisa, 71
    Loula A, 48
    Lulu, 58
    Sandrum, 116
HENDLEY
    Child of C M, 34
HENLEY
    Eva, 63
    Infant of M and Susan, 72
    Lucious, 86
HENLY
    Chas M, 126
HEWLETT
    George, 45
    Louisa, 71
    Mary, 42
    Thursday, 76
HEWS
    Arthur, 63
HICKMAN
    Ida, 93
    Roland, 124

HICKS
    Amie B, 80
    Burrell, 54
    Eliza, 89
    Lizzie, 31, 89
    Thos, 59
HILL
    Alton, 136
    Blanche, 101
    Charley, 51
    Elizabeth B, 136
    Ellen, 37
    Estell, 74
    John E, 110
    Mary A, 105
    Pecar(?), 129
    Rosalia, 58
HILLARD
    Amanda, 119
    Sarah E, 118
HILTON
    Amie R, 49
    Clara, 74
    Elmira, 80
    Florence E, 117
    Fred, 67
    Herman, 109
    Martha E, 67
HIRE
    Johnson, 89
HIX
    Dolley, 67
    Infant of Thomas, 29
HOBSON
    Estelle, 63, 131
    Lillie May, 131
    Oscar, 114
    Willie, 131
HOLIONBER
    Jno R, 75
HOLMES
    Alma, 99
    Jennie, 44
    John Henry, 28
    Johnson, 62

HOLMES (cont.)
  Mary J, 121
HOPES
  Alexander Benj, 105
HORKS
  Catharine, 77
HOUSE
  Judge, 80
HOWARD
  Catherine, 84
  Louisa, 134
  Mary, 93
  Wm H, 69
HOWEL
  Rachael, 95
HOWELL
  Charles, 62
HOWLET
  Infants of T and wife, 89
  Maria, 116
  Peter, 117
  Richard, 93
HOWLETT
  Florence, 54
  Jennie, 29
  Sarah R, 50
  Souissa(?), 136
  Wilson, 137
HOWWARD
  Annie May, 60
HUDLETT
  Abbey, 45
HUDSON
  Infant of Mary, 65
HUGHES
  Bessie, 43
  Earnest, 115
  Genevive, 30
  Ida Jane, 33
  Nellie, 131
HUNT
  Bettie, 46
HUNTER
  Charity, 79
  Infant of Sallie, 51

HURT
  Jennie, 91
IRVINE
  Elvira, 97
  Leslie, 111
  William, 68
JACKSON
  Antony, 78
  Chas, 49, 51
  Crenshaw, 105
  Eliza Jane, 111
  Emma, 62
  Fletcher, 133
  Francis, 108
  Henry, 27
  Horace, 106
  Infant of Eliza, 112
  Infant of Louis, 86
  Johnson, 31
  Martha, 30
  Mary, 49, 93
  Mary E, 50, 60
  Nelson, 78
  Ola, 82
  Rebecca, 31
  Roy De Witt, 132
  Rufus, 89
  Ruth, 62
  Susan A, 49, 51
  Sydney, 93
  Thelma, 122
  Thomas, 85
  Wm, 108
JAMES
  Annie L, 135
  Louise, 109
  Robert H, 127
  Tomy, 113
JASPER
  Cuffy Jr, 122
  Mary Alia, 69–70
JEETER
  Henry, 115

164 Richmond, Virginia, Mt. Olivet Cemetery Register

JEFFERSON
  Chas, 122
  Davis, 94
  Ellen Joseph, 34
  Mrs Anna, 113
JENKINS
  Isham, 40
  Julia, 38
  Willie L, 92
JESER
  Joshua, 26
JOHNSON
  Alex, 134
  Alexander, 100
  Amelia Ann, 71
  Anna, 63
  Charles H, 75
  Edwd, 103
  Ella, 82
  Fanny, 98
  Grant, 34
  H I, 69
  Henry, 125
  Hire, 89
  Indianna, 38
  Infant of Rosa, 108
  J Sarah, 92
  James, 50, 58
  Jas R, 110
  Jennie, 81
  John, 72
  Joseph, 106
  Josephine, 94
  Julia, 43
  Julia Ann, 31
  Laray, 85
  Lelia, 95
  Lewis, 114
  Lillie, 103
  Louisa, 101
  Lousa, 114
  Lucy Ann, 103
  Margaret E, 41
  Mary, 30
  Mary Royall, 111

JOHNSON (cont.)
  Nancy, 47
  Pearl A, 39
  Richard, 34
  Robert, 33
  Robt, 135
  Ruth, 43
  S Sarah, 92
  Susan, 68
  Susan E, 43
  Tom H, 55
  Walker, 118
  Wm E, 88
  Wm H, 87
JOHNSTON
  Nannie, 42
JONATHAN
  John, 29
JONES
  Agnes R, 93
  Albert, 45
  Armstead, 26
  Benj, 133
  Charles, 39
  Cl, 105
  Dorothea, 118
  Eliza, 38
  Herbert R, 74
  Infant of Pinkee, 129
  Jackson, 25
  Jacob, 102
  Jas, 134
  Jennie, 111
  Judy, 38
  Louisa, 132
  Lucy, 69
  Mariah, 84
  Mary, 82
  Nancy, 134
  Nancy B, 81
  Ony, 126
  Perry W, 64
  Richard I, 90
  Robert, 99
  S J, 138

JONES (cont.)
　Sarah, 105
　Willie Robert, 104
KEELING
　Infant of Mariah, 37
KELLY
　Infant of Nora, 90
KEYE
　Stephen, 100
KEYES
　Calvin, 82
KEYLEY
　Bernard, 32
KEYO
　Infant, 41
KEYS
　Ruby, 125
　Stephen, 46
KINDER
　Lelia, 107
KING
　Caroline, 30
　Hazel (male), 129
　Luellie, 88
　Sidney, 89
　Taylor, 34
KNIGHT
　Infant of Jack, 70
KUK
　Mary, 81
LANGSTON
　Geo, 92
LAWSON
　Emma, 40
　Julia, 126
LEE
　Edward, 131
　Josie, 83
LEWIS
　Eliza, 122
　Sarah, 30
　Wm, 102
　Wm A, 102

LIPSCOMB
　Eliza, 48
　Green, 105
LIRTHEY
　Henry, 80
LITTLE
　Arthur, 129
LIVES
　Elizabeth, 34
LOCKET
　Iseah, 119
LOGAN
　Al---, 62
　Chas, 57
　Infant of Mary, 59, 115
　Infant of Sarah, 54
　J Louise, 114
　John H Jr, 136
　Josephine, 53
　Madeline, 131
　Nancy, 108
　Robie, 134
　Zelina, 124
LOUISE
　Roubert (male), 64
LOVELACE
　Andrew, 41
　Chas, 38
　John H, 128
　M, 89
MANN
　Charles, 42
　Georgianer, 67
　Nancy, 36
　Robert I, 91
　Thos H, 106
MARSHALL
　Frances, 126
　Matilda, 93
　Rebecca, 78
MARTIN
　Mary, 135
MARTON
　Mariha, 67

MASON
  Delphia, 92
  Estelle, 76
  Henry, 135
  Henry Spence, 137
  Lee, 76
  Mary, 97
  Sarah E, 78
MASSE
  E, 72
MATHEWS
  Child of Hanna, 29
  William, 87
MAYO
  Aggie, 71
  Annie, 27
  Arromento, 28
  D Willie, 62
  George E, 27
  Jane, 32
  Mary Ellen, 31
  Nicholas, 73
  Rosa, 64
  William, 27
  William E, 40
  William R, 28
MAYR
  Jessie, 94
MCKENZIE
  Kate, 108
MEADE
  Bennie, 88
MECKANS
  Fanny, 56
MEEBORN
  L J, 46
MEEKINS
  David, 131
MELLER
  Sam'l, 48
MEYO
  Ellenora, 132
  Martha, 124
  Sarah, 99

MICKENS
  Albert, 128
  Son of A and Judia, 76
MILES
  John, 103
MILHERES
  Rebecca, 82
MILLER
  Adelia, 81
  Anni, 71
  Elijah, 25
  Elsie, 128
  Fanny, 59
  Giles, 46
  Kate, 76
  Monero, 100
  Nelson, 77
  Ocolia, 60
  Olivia, 114
  Percel, 102
  Peter, 104
  Victoria, 34
MINGLETON
  Ellen, 25
  Walker, 33
MINUS
  G R, 130
MIRE
  Mary E, 104
MITCHEL
  America, 122
MONGER
  Peter, 79
MONROE
  James R, 32
  Thos, 109
MONTAGUE
  Infant of Billie, 79
  Infant of Carrie, 71
  Martha, 135
  Mary, 128
  Wm, 68
MOON
  Lucy L, 98

MOORE
  Adam, 30
  Gertrude, 110
  John, 94
  Lelia, 26
MOOSBY
  Addie, 56
  Alfred, 56
  Jessee, 85
MOOSLEY
  Robert, 132
MORRIS
  Archer, 38
  Eddie Nelson, 25
  Emma, 26
MORRISON
  Ella W, 47
MORRISS
  Tandy, 28
MORTON
  Amanda, 89
  Amy, 57
  Catharine, 68
  Infant of Tom and Mary, 87
  Rebecca, 38
  Robert, 51, 136
  Thomas, 86
MOSBY
  Arthur H, 119
  Chas, 109
  Lucy Jane, 73
  Page, 129
  Powhatan, 72
  Robt, 34
MOSELEY
  Chas, 131
  Eliza, 119
MOSELY
  Infant of H and wife, 83
MOSS
  Charity Ann, 85
MUNFORD
  Annie L, 91
  Biunthel, 118
  Earnest C, 127

MUNROE
  Jane, 59
MURPHY
  Fred, 81
MURRAY
  Gracie, 101
MURRY
  Antony, 86
  Chas, 86
  Emma, 92
  Marie, 99
MUSE
  Elvina, 93
  Infant of Lotie, 70
  Joseph, 69
NARH
  Abram, 63
NASH
  Chas Duval, 78
NELSON
  Charlie, 85
  Cyrus, 68
  Frank Sr, 56
  Harrat, 89
  Sophy, 91
OLPHIN
  Granville, 100
ORANGE
  Tom, 84
PAGE
  Infant of Mary, 80, 84
  Mary, 88
  Mosby, 129
PAINE
  Clarence, 42
PARAHAM
  Martha, 127
PARSON
  Jas, 91
PASCALL
  Robert, 115
PATTERSON
  Ruth, 107
  Saml, 109

PENNOCK
  Jas, 120
PERRY
  Jas, 122
  Montessa, 73
PETERSON
  Elvira, 49
PETTERSON
  Peter, 98
PEUCHAUM
  Bell, 57
PINCHAM
  Dan'l, 111
PLEASANTS
  Howard, 133
  Infant of Wm, 132
POINDEXTER
  Louisa, 27
POLK
  Lawson, 125
POLLARD
  Annie, 126
  Lelia, 122
  Willie, 133
POOL
  Thomas, 67
POPE
  Jas, 94
PORTER
  Willie, 49
POTTS
  Thomas, 35
POWEL
  Arabella, 119
  Cora B, 97
  Eugene, 104
  Melissie, 96
POWELL
  Chas, 84
  Gladys, 122
  Jeff, 80
  Mary, 127
  Sissie, 99
  Willis, 40

PRICE
  Geo Allen, 118
  Isac, 59
  James, 63
  Joseph, 97
  L L, 78
  Rosa Bell, 96
PRIDE
  Bessie, 118
  Helen L, 130
PROSSER
  Nellie, 98
PRYMAN
  Infant of Addie, 72
PUGH
  Florence, 122
  Roach A, 126
QUARLES
  Peyton, 123
QUAWLS
  Samuel, 57
RANDALL
  Georgianna, 78
RANDOLPH
  Bing, 77
  Georgianna, 99
  Henry, 30
  Howard L, 118
  Infant of Emily, 83
  James, 48
  Lewis, 35
  Lizzie, 66
  Mary E, 30, 61
  Rachael, 40
  Robert P R, 66
  Ruth, 114
  W R, 43
  Walter, 29
  Wilson, 34
RAWLINGS
  Infant of John, 39
READE
  Lewis, 36

REED
   Isaac, 48
   Wm, 88
REID
   Henry, 129
REVELY
   George, 34
RHONE
   M Eva, 103
RICHARDSON
   Grove, 130
   Infant of Mary, 83
   Norville, 120
   W, 87
   Wm, 117
RICHMOND
   Smith, 106
RIDLEY
   Richard, 26
RIEVES
   Madaline, 66
RILEY
   Infant of Adelaide, 85
ROANE
   Daniel, 48
   John, 112
   Kizziah, 65
   Ora Roane, 121
ROBERSON
   Jula, 63
ROBERTSON
   Cyphus, 119
   Dilsey, 128
   Elizabeth, 44
   Jas, 68
   Pittman, 65
   Priscilla, 44
ROBINS
   Elizabeth, 29
ROBINSON
   Beverly, 26
   Chas, 120
   Clara, 43
   Coleman, 49, 62
   Coleman Sr, 62

ROBINSON (cont.)
   David, 136
   Delia, 75
   Dora, 124
   Elizabeth, 112
   Emily, 39
   Emma, 61
   Eva, 67
   Floyd, 87, 127
   Fred, 135
   Granville, 94, 100
   Henry, 46
   Infant of Lelia, 93
   Infant of M and S, 66
   Irly, 137
   James, 44
   Jas, 125
   John, 133
   Joseph Henry, 127
   Laura, 125
   Lelia, 114
   Linwood, 137
   Margurette M, 137
   Pashal, 48
   Rosabella, 104
   Sarah, 50
ROCK
   Fannie, 105
   Fred, 132
ROLLINGS
   Maria, 111
ROLLINS
   Ella, 61
   Infant of Jno, 38
ROSE
   Virginia, 114
ROSS
   Chas A, 55, 58
   Edie, 36
   James E, 55
   Jane, 99
   Jas E, 58
   Mary B, 78
   Rosa, 102
   Ruth E, 72

Richmond, Virginia, Mt. Olivet Cemetery Register

ROUBERT
  Louise (male), 64
ROYALL
  Jennie, 111
ROYSTER
  Jas, 127
RUDOLPH
  Martha, 56
  Wm Henry, 60
RUFFIN
  Infant of Liddia, 47
  Lilly, 82
RUSSLE
  Robert, 133
SALLEY
  Infant of Henry and Nancy, 71
SAUNDERS
  Charles, 64
  Emma, 83
  James H, 56
  Lee, 77
  Mary, 36, 43
SAVAGE
  Lucy, 134
SCHOUREN
  Aaron, 68
SCOTT
  Bessie, 135
  Elvira, 50
  Julia B, 97
  Katie, 87
  Mary Jane, 77
SEUREOEL(?)
  Lelia G, 123
SHARP
  Anthony, 84
SHAW
  Ophelia, 120
SHELTON
  Georganna, 91
SHERRON
  Thomas, 123
SIMMON
  Mad, 64

SIMMONS
  Louisea, 124
  Mary, 76
  Richard, 57
SKIPWITH
  Ora B, 137
SLAUGHTER
  Infant of T B, 88
SMITH
  Alberta, 40
  Amanda, 95
  Andrew, 42
  Anni, 72
  Charles, 86
  Delia, 33
  Eddie, 101
  Florence, 116
  Florence G, 113
  Frank, 113
  Helen L, 61
  Infant of Bertha, 33
  Infant of Delia, 29
  Infant of Lizzie, 80
  Infant of Wm, 31
  James, 36
  Joseph, 66
  Leray, 35
  Lewis, 97
  Lizzie, 89
  Maria, 133
  Mary, 32, 44
  Mary E, 71
  Mary L, 123
  Pelio, 131
  Peter, 57
  Richmond, 106
  Robert, 27
  Robt, 42
  Royall, 134
  Sinmord, 86
  Synthy, 127
  Wm, 35, 39
  Wm H, 69
SNEED
  Lizzie, 118

SOUTHALL
  Marie, 53
  Oti, 75
STAPLES
  Carrie, 83
  Estelle, 104
  Johnson, 82
STARKE
  Berta, 88
STEPHENY
  Matilda, 56
STERLING
  Elizabeth, 122
STEWART
  Willie, 30
STOKES
  Berta, 133
  Mary S(?), 66
STOWE
  Cora, 49–50
STRATTEN
  Alexander, 95
STRAYGHTER
  Infant of T B, 88
STREET
  George, 121
STREETS
  A, 92
  Harry, 51
STRINGFELLOW
  Peter, 84
STRONN
  Julia, 29
STUART
  Infant of Emma, 80
STULTZ
  Norman, 120
SULLEY
  Henry, 111
SUTHERLAND
  Miles, 56
SWOON
  Aaron, 29
SYDNOR
  Frank, 37

TALLIFERRO
  Curtis, 132
TATUM
  Ama, 41
TAYLOR
  Alice, 42
  Archer, 133
  Arthur, 113
  Catharine, 123
  Edna, 132
  Geo, 44
  Geo Henry, 120
  Infant of Alice, 37
  Infant of Archer and wife, 93
  Infant of Mary, 32
  Jas, 33
  Jno, 87
  Lucy, 38
  Paulina, 109
  Robert, 90
  Walter, 119
TERRY
  Eliza, 119
THOMALSON
  Garland, 67
THOMAS
  Alice P, 60
  Armstead, 84
  Charles, 60
  Elizabeth, 60
  Infant of Rebecca, 45
  Jessee, 99
  Ruth, 46
  Wm, 79
THOMPSON
  Blanche, 43
  Charles, 44
  Eddie, 105
  Ernest, 74
  Francis W, 39
  Laura A, 51
  W Y, 124
THOMSON
  Chas W, 63

THREAT
  Infant of Henry and Mary, 112
THREET
  Infant of H and M, 101
TILERY
  Robt P, 125
TIMBERLAKE
  L J, 90
TINSLEY
  Infant of Geo and wife, 108
  Leroy, 129
TOMPKINS
  Maggie, 50
TRENT
  Infant of Anna B, 91
  James, 32
  Matilda, 129
TUBBS
  John H, 100
TURNER
  Annie, 26
  Charlotte, 97
  Eugen, 73
  Granville, 52
  Infants of Magr, 51
  Mary D, 98
  Wm, 85
TURPIN
  Armelia, 88
  Edmond, 107
  Edmund, 36
TWINE
  Charlie, 47
  Elsey, 90
TYLER
  Osca, 73
UNKNOWN, 33, 52–53, 55–56, 61,
  68, 78–79, 82–83, 86, 89, 103
  (12y Male), 30
  Infant, 25, 28, 35, 42–43, 45, 47,
    49, 60, 73–74, 79, 121
  Mariah, 28
  No name listed, 38
  Pauper, 69

VALENTINE
  Eva, 54, 58
  Martha A, 54, 58
VAUGHN
  Infant of Mary, 77
VENABLE
  Elvira, 97
  Infant of Mattie, 85
  Rebecca, 68
WADDELE
  Clara, 130
WADDELLE
  Ira, 104
WAKEFIELD
  J W, 138
WALKE
  Thos, 98
WALKER
  Cynthy, 28
  Infant of W and wife, 121
  Joseph, 50
  Lucinda, 87
  Margaret E, 32
  Patsey, 42
WALLACE
  William E, 46
WALLER
  C L, 134
WALTHALL
  Chas H, 112
  Woodson, 47
WARD
  Mary, 59
WARREN
  Wm, 70
WASHINGTON
  Betsy Ann, 98
  Delphia, 90
  George, 33
  Howard Lee, 107
  Jno Thomas, 33
  Parthemia, 27
  Robert, 133
  Wilhart, 109

Richmond, Virginia, Mt. Olivet Cemetery Register 173

WATKINS
  Betty, 39
  Francis W, 35
  Julia, 35
  Peter, 57
  Sallie, 30
WATSON
  Arthur, 126
  Richard, 79
WELLS
  Lewis, 84
WEST
  Adelia, 111
  Catharine, 68
  Jno, 103
WHITE
  A, 58
  Amy, 65
  Ann, 50
  Charlotte, 113
  Infant of Amelia, 60
  Infant of Edwd, 45
  Jacob, 35
  James T, 40
  Joh, 65
  Leroy, 130
  Lucy, 44
  Sallie, 134
  Sam, 75
WHITEHEAD
  John, 121
WHITLOCK
  H H, 51
WHITMON
  Infant of John, 32
WHITTEKER
  Jessee, 76
WILDER
  Lucile A, 106
WILEY
  Aubrey, 99
  Bertie, 55
  Geo, 40
  Sallie, 117

WILKINSON
  Daniel, 54
  Infant of Daniel, 37
  Infant of Mattie, 55
  Susan, 25, 34
WILLBOR
  Clarence, 53
WILLIAM
  Infant of Jno and wife, 96
WILLIAMS
  Belle, 86
  Bessie May, 71
  Clara, 116
  Cora, 72
  Elizabeth, 47
  Infant of Bettie, 52
  James, 44
  Lethia, 131
  Mary, 127
  Ruth, 95
  Susan, 95
  Tom, 121
WILLSON
  Emma, 115
WINFRED
  Wm, 124
WINFREE
  Charlotte, 132
  Estelle, 66
  Fanny, 58
  Ida, 61
  John S, 30
  Rebecca, 55
WINGFIELD
  Florence, 82
WINSTON
  Bansey, 99
  Edwd, 128
  Willie, 126
WIRT
  Nannie, 64
WMITH
  Infant of W E L, 113

WOODSON
    Elanora, 42
    Spencer, 44
WOODY
    Isam, 98
WOOLDRADGE
    Maurace, 40
    Richard M, 36
WOOLDRIDGE
    Jas C, 84
    Richard, 61
    Richard I, 47
    Wm R, 26
WOOLRIDGE
    Cornelius, 100
    Samuel, 65
WOOLRIDIGE
    Martha, 137

WOOTEN
    Ella, 73
WORSHAM
    Margaret E, 118
    Thos B, 39
    William C, 45
WRENN
    Joshua, 99
WRIGHT
    Alsey, 81
    Colon, 63
WYATT
    Mathews, 128
YOUNG
    Anna Bell, 94
    Elizabeth, 74, 118

www.ingramcontent.com/pod-product-compliance
Lightning Source LLC
Chambersburg PA
CBHW050633160426
43194CB00010B/1652